THE UNDIMINISHED LINK
FORTY YEARS AND BEYOND

Victor Waldron

To Fusion
Best Regards
N H Lo...

Published in Great Britain by Hansib Publications in 2007

Hansib Publications Limited
London & Hertfordshire, UK

Email: info@hansib-books.com
Website: www.hansib-books.com

ISBN 1 870518 82 9

Cover designed by Stefan Brazzo
Printed by Progress Press Ltd, Malta

THE AUTHOR

Victor Waldron was born in Plaisance, Guyana, on 3rd March 1935. He was a pupil of St Paul's Anglican School.

After graduating, he gained employment at the Ogle sugar plantation as a clerical officer. He subsequently moved onto the workshop as an engineer, for eight years.

On arrival in Great Britain in 1959, he was employed by London Underground and later by the Post Office until retirement.

He has shown much enthusiasm towards writing throughout his life and, as a hobby, it has always been a source of great enjoyment. He initially focused on several television scripts and poetry, which are yet to be published.

His memoirs are published here for the first time.

ACKNOWLEDGEMENTS

The greatest gift of mankind is meeting and associating with people of the highest esteem. To that end I have been truly blessed and most fortunate.

Today I take the opportunity to express grateful thanks to a few who have given my life true meaning and fulfilment.

Firstly my life long friend Fitroy Headley whose energy and support was beyond the bounds of mere friendship. He gave his time and effort unselfishly and assisted me hugely in helping to fulfil my goal.

Keith Gordon – my brother-in-law – also showed remarkable patience and his constructive advice has helped considerably in making the venture a success.

So too are my son Colin and daughters Karen and Claire whose encouragement and persistence kept me going when my spirit and enthusiasm wavered.

Most of all my gracious thanks to my wonderful wife whose tacit but solid support did so much to keep my focus and interest alive. How could I have survived without her warm smile and those stimulating cups of tea which was always very welcome.

Finally to my other friends who have kept faith in me constantly over the years. They helped urge me to achieve my dream to the very end. Special mention to Danny, Newton, Fred, Chris, Larry, Lennox, Felix and Derek my son-in-law, to name a few, and many, many more.

You all have been an inspiration to me and for that I shall always be truly grateful.

Victor Waldron
September 2006

CONTENTS

MY EARLY YEARS IN PLAISANCE, GUYANA

In one of life's glorious moments on this magnificent journey of ours, comes a thought or idea that gives meaning to our existence. Perhaps the most poignant moment of my life was making the conscious decision to leave the country of my birth for England. Travelling abroad was never a preoccupation of mine. England, America, Canada or any part of Europe for that matter, were simply faraway places where academics and professionals visited, some to further their aims, some returning after accomplishing theirs and since I was not in any of these categories, my natural contemplation to leave Guyana was basically non-existent. I was employed, enjoyed a relatively decent social existence with many friends. Consequently, life was generally acceptable.

Plaisance, where I was born in 1935, was a delightful little village and a very happy place. Happiness is of course relative but living in a community that was enriched by sincere people and genuine friendships made a remarkable difference to all of us.

My parents were very strict, especially my Dad and so we functioned under a different ethos to what exists today. We were a British colony. Our lives anyway were never in a straight jacket. My favourite person was my mother, with whom I was always able to obtain favours from and invariably, managed to gain the upper hand. That, I believed, was because she understood me better than my brothers and sisters. It was often expressed that I was her favourite but that thought never crossed my mind. We were an immediate family of eight plus six half brothers and sisters. Perhaps at a glance, one would have noticed that the culture of keeping the family to a minimum was not in place.

My parents were not very well off but our status and our circumstances were far healthier to many in the neighbourhood. Our life there was quite simple but what was important, we did the simple things well.

My Dad, who was a teacher in his early years, was forced to augment his salary – due to the low wages – by acquiring a skill as a jeweller. In fact, he became so successful at doing so; he eventually opted for a full time career in the jewellery trade. As a result, not only did he do sterling work in that field, he was able to train many people in that particular art.

I was a Sixth Former when my Dad passed away in 1947, leaving a huge financial imbalance to our household. For me personally, it was unfortunate that I was never able to know him better. He was a quiet, decent and respectable member of our community but he was never truly a friend to us. He was Dad; and in that era, that was all that was necessary. It was then that my mother, faced by the circumstances around us, demonstrated the depth of her character, strength of her spirit and ambition to achieve the best for her family. Through thrift, amazing hard work and a robust desire to succeed, she was able to maintain a decent living standard for us and an existence that can be regarded in many ways as quite adequate. However, the opportunities I had hoped for and dreamt about were now in serious jeopardy. My secondary education was now on hold and even though my Mum insisted on me having further education, I knew that she would be doing so in a manner detrimental to our life style. To impose a strain of such dimension on her was not something I was prepared to accommodate – she had done enough for us already and I for one did not believe I should push her to any extremes.

Our community, as I indicated before was an attractive place and many people were encouraged to visit. Our Saturday nights were very much a jamboree; everything lit up and everyone came out simply to take in what was on offer. We drank *mauby* – a local brew – ices, drinks, peanuts and generally did what young people did; having a good time. In the grand scheme of things, I did not envisage leaving the community for any other place.

ENTERING THE WORLD OF WORK

Right next to our village was a thriving sugar plantation called Ogle. It was a leading work area that employed a vast number of people from far and wide. That being so, Plaisance became a vital and very important area for those who lived distances away and home to a great many who decided to reside there.

I entered into employment as a clerk at the estate but I was not entirely happy working as a clerical officer. My greatest wish and my first priority was always to become a mechanical engineer. Watching my colleagues in the workshop covered in grease was a source of attraction and even delight to me. How I longed to become a 'grease monkey' like them. One year later I transferred as an apprentice into the Internal Combustion department – steam - where I stayed for eight years, never accomplishing that yearning of mine ever to become a mechanic. However, there was a measure of compensation moving into the workshop. It was there that I came into contact with numerous friends. Elan McLennan was one of them. The only downside was meeting and working with George Stayman. He was my boss and the one responsible for our section.

Back in the village and somewhere in the distant past, I encountered and became attached to someone whose mutual interest and compatibility were so akin to mine that an immediate bond between us became apparent. Our friendship gathered pace as the years passed simply because of its very nature. It was solid, consistent and enduring, and it has remained steadfast to this present time. His name is Fitzroy Headley, together we shared a glorious past, especially in the things of interest, such as cricket, music, films, dancing but more importantly singing. We were in fact an integral part of a robust and healthy bunch of young villagers who shared many activities together. The fairer sex whose beauty and charm were very much in abundance gave us every reason to excel in what we did to gain their special attention. I played cricket at an extreme high level. I was also a member of the village youth team who took their sports seriously and played to the highest calibre.

We also danced and how we loved to dance. I cannot say this with any arrogance or boast, but there is a certain uniqueness about the way Guyanese dance. In my humble experience, I cannot remember any other Caribbean Island that dance the way we do. Its origin I know very little of except to say it is a cross between the British with a huge Latin American flavour, if I am to express it, I would say it is a ballroom dance with a very serious Guyanese attitude. To observe a skilled couple floating across the dance floor; swinging, swaying, turning and twisting to the strains of the once famous 'Washboards' or 'Syncopators' two of our outstanding orchestra's of that era was really something to behold. My own skills for the wonderful art form were seriously limited, but what I may have lacked in talent I could not be faulted for enthusiasm and boundless energy. It was all amazingly good fun!

As a singing group we assembled every evening mainly to hone our harmonious skills to its optimum. We were also privilege to have lived in a golden era of singers and entertainers such as Nat King Cole, Perry Como, Johnny Mathias, Jimmy Greaves, Roy Hamilton, Sam Cook and many, many more that were both fabulous and stimulating artistes. However, the group that influenced our own development was none other than the irrepressible Everley Brothers. Their music and style was simply unique. Not only did they give us tremendous pleasure they were a group that we hoped to emulate. Our rendition of 'All I have to do is Dream' was never on par with the group but we simply enjoyed singing it.

Our Friday evenings were reserved exclusively for the grand purpose of another hobby 'the cinema'. We derived tremendous pleasures from watching a good movie. Cycling as we did to the city, (approximately six miles from the village); stopping off for a peanut punch and *puri* at a popular eating place called '*Ferraz*'. Taking in a feature film from one of the main cinemas such as the Globe, Astor, Metropole or the Strand brings back great memories. Returning home and battling against the wind gave the ride a very competitive edged and there was absolutely no glory of being last of the bunch. That carried a tag of failure, which was never ever forgotten. Nevertheless it was all part of the fun that we had, adding in no small measure to the grandness and fulfilment of our youth.

We still remember those wonderful years for the sheer joy and happiness they brought to us. Today we can look back on our youthful years with much satisfaction and reminisce on things and events that still run richly in our veins.

I was a pupil of St. Paul's School and as a consequence became a member of the Anglican Church. I can only surmise that my father's influence in this matter was paramount. My mother was born in Paramaribo, Suriname; she was a Catholic by birth and may have crossed over merely to accommodate my dad who was an Anglican. The family dynamics of that period meant, it was a man's prerogative in deciding on matters of importance and it was usually the woman's place to fall in line. What was obvious and very much a reality also, was that as a British colony, the levers of power and control were firmly in the hands of Europeans. Be it governmental, business or matters of civic importance. It would therefore hardly surprise anyone to imagine that our priest was an Englishman called Father Salmon; someone who was more renowned for his acts of intimidation rather than his sermons. His entire manner was confrontational which resulted in the congregation being more in fear than in union with him, and even though I was a naïve youth at that time, I firmly believed that he was not a suitable candidate of 'the cloth.' He was very grumpy and mean-spirited, attributes that were not compatible with what I expected from a holy man.

The yard of his rectory was littered with fruit trees and it was always a temptation for youngsters to gain access in order to obtain some of it but his yapping dogs, his servant but most importantly, the Holy Father's bad temper, kept everyone at bay. I recall two very brave lads defying the odds and helping themselves to some of his fruits and they were clever enough to avoid being caught by the reverend father, who chased them with a stick. When on the safe side of danger, one of the lads shouted out teasingly and somewhat triumphantly; "Father Salmon it's only a few fruits".

The Reverend, red in the face and flushed with anger replied; "Father Salmon? I'll make sardines of you if you ever cross this yard again". That showed in no uncertain way that he lacked generosity of spirit. His demeanour provoked fear, not only for me but many of the villagers who came in contact with him. As was the case with the fruits, he would rather have them fall and rot on the ground than share them with others.

My first and only encounter with the Holy Father was a bitter and most unfortunate experience. One that shattered my innocence and brought to the fore an awareness that was not in evidence before. It was to do with the dreaded business of church dues.

Church dues were one of the most important matters that needed to be addressed. Failure to comply with the request for payment at a given time, carried with it great distress to those who were unable or unwilling to do so. The stigma of the Holy Father announcing the names of those in default on the pulpit on Sundays, meant some of the congregation were forced to make sacrifices of tremendous importance in order to be on the safe side of that ordeal.

I recall my mother sending me to pay her church dues one day. The vestry was closed, so I proceeded to his rectory. The dogs were in full chorus, barking and rushing to the gate. The servant seeing me there enquired what my business was; I informed her that I needed to pay my mother's church dues. She beckoned to me to come in and insisted on me doing so even though the dogs were at their fiercest. Declining to enter the yard without protection, I attracted Father Salmon's attention. He looked out of the window, a man clearly upset by the noise of the barking dogs, and asked, "Are you coming in or are you prepared to stand there all day?"

I stood my ground, not wanting to become a victim of dog bites – "Your dogs father" I said, "I am afraid of them."

He waived his hand impatiently; "You either come in or get your little black ass from my gate" was his retort.

For a brief moment I looked at this most uncharitable man and felt a tinge of pity for him. It was the first time that someone had used the colour of my skin as a form of rebuke. It may seem simplistic but up until then, the idea of colour or race was something I never gave consideration to. People were just people and although it was obvious that some people were white and others were not, it was never an issue until now. It was certainly a rude awakening for me. What was unfortunate in my estimation; what the reverend had done was just using his 'whiteness' to devalue those people like myself who were not.

I turned away and returned home to my mother, telling her the story and informing her that I would never 'cross that man's path' again. She understood. My refusal was not out of disrespect for her; it was simply that I was determined to keep well away from someone for whom I was now sure that I had not the slightest bit of goodwill.

Very soon after, my mother returned to her true faith. Needless to say, I was only too pleased to follow in her footsteps. Nevertheless that experience with the Holy Father is not one I am ever likely to forget.

My years at the plantation, under the stewardship of Stayman can hardly be considered enlightened or enhancing. His philosophy, by and large, was to accentuate the virtues of the Englishman, without due care or consideration for himself or the 'lesser breed' as he would call us.

I was a young man and very impressionable and although the theories he expounded were hardly taken seriously, he managed in some ways to influence my thinking, which undoubtedly clouded my outlook. Example, it is said has a transient power. That saying I believe to be true. Unfortunately, his was an example I could well do without. It rendered me somewhat vulnerable and unprepared to face the new venture I was about to undertake.

CIRCUMSTANCES THAT INFLUENCED IMMIGRATION FROM GUYANA IN THE 50s

Things were beginning to change, however, and a new political shape was about to emerge. Guyana had only just enjoyed its first non-colonial government. The People's Progressive Party had won a landslide election victory. Hopes and expectations were sky high. We had acquired adult suffrage from our colonial masters and that election heralded much hope for the Guianese people. Alas it was not to be. Within months of winning, the constitution was suspended (9 October 1953) and was replaced by an interim government. Governor Savage, who represented the colonial interest, took the view that the elected members were unfit to run the Country – calling them "An unscrupulous bunch" – and with orders from London suspended the reign and with it the hopes of a great many people. It must be said, however, that Guyanese enjoyed a high standard of living under colonial rule. The level of education especially, was considered the highest around the Caribbean Basin and society under colonial rule was chiselled along the same lines and was in fact a reflection of "the Mother Country", England. Local mannerisms and habits apart, we were a carbon copy of those who ruled us.

Being the only English speaking country in South America, naturally English was our first language. English history taught us about the exploits of Nelson and Drake. Reading about Dickens and Shakespeare was as natural as eating breadfruit. The Union Jack, which we flew with pride, was never a problem as were our passports – again British – our Parliament – Westminster style. Our churches and even our newspaper – The Thompson Group informed us of "good old England". The highest point of the day was perhaps listening to the BBC News – considered second to none.

I was ten years old when I became a serious fan of Surrey Cricket Club and a year later my love affair with Arsenal Football Club commenced and has remained with me faithfully to this day. Armed with so much of the colonial past or rather the British way of life, I thought it would be relatively easy – or so I imagined – making the transition from Guyana to England. The reality of that experience is as disappointing as it is unfortunate. On arrival in England we were perceived in the main as uneducated individuals, unintelligent and incapable of knowing or understanding even basic things. In a word we were just stupid people. That concept has remained constant – though perhaps to a lesser extent- to this day.

Although Guyana enjoyed a fairly good standard of living at the time, there was nevertheless a high level of unemployment. It was the era of the 'Fair Skin' people. If you were fair and a practising catholic, your chances of success exceeded those who were dark. By and large, people benefited that way. My ambition was to become a mechanical engineer and even though I was doing an apprenticeship in steam engineering, it was not what I desired. It was then that I started a diploma course with the Los Angeles School of Motoring, which I finally completed after my arrival in England.

The Country's mood had begun to change dramatically. Things were taking on a new perspective. The call by the British Government to come to the 'Mother Country' created a frenzied interest everywhere and although it was not an exodus at the time, that was not long in coming. There was a labour shortage in England and almost everyone knew someone who had gone and was doing well. It became for many, the only option. I prided myself on thinking independently and the mass hysteria, which pervaded the society, had nothing to do with me. My agenda was different. Should I leave the country, it would be for America where I would finish my course, work there for five years, ten at the most and be back in Guyana.

Elan McLennan, a colleague of mine and someone whom I always admired, was the first person to introduce the idea of leaving Guyana for England. He was always in the company of older men and showed great maturity. We worked alongside each other and spoke frequently. It was during one of those discussions that he revealed his thoughts to me of leaving for England. Guyana offered very little scope for people so he argued and that for me was a constructive piece of advice. It was the only way of fulfilling my ambition. One which I readily accepted.

The person who inspired me most at that time was my mother. She was my guiding light in matters of importance and so I found the task of revealing my plans to her and more especially to ask her to finance it; most unpleasant. I discussed the matter with Elan who told me that his mind had been made up and should I take the decision to go, he would like us to make the journey together. Perhaps, that more than anything else was the spur I needed to make the venture. The thought of travelling on my own to this strange land was just as daunting as working with 'blue-eyed white people' as my old boss Stayman would describe them. He constantly narrated to us or to anyone who would listen, about 'white people' and how different they were. Needless to say, he held them in awe. It was manifestly clear that his self-esteem was extremely low. To him white people represented superiority and greatness; black people in his eyes were mere ordinary mortals. Small wonder that when the chief engineer, white of course, paid his customary visit to the plant where we worked, Stayman would be seen visibly shaking with fear until his departure.

The experience of Stayman, although not unique at the time – there were others like him- clearly left self-doubt in my mind about Europeans. Being young and with hardly any in- depth political knowledge or sense of history, except European history, the general innocence of mind that things invented or created were always done by white people incorrectly and unwittingly lent credence to the superior and inferior factor. It was not difficult to become a victim of such an erroneous philosophy. The adage that 'ignorance is bliss' is open to serious questioning. To be blissfully stupid is most unfortunate.

My mother gave me the encouragement that I needed. Fully aware of the circumstances in Guyana, she conceded. Although it was a heart wrenching exercise, it was ultimately the right choice to make. She told me that sentiments must not impede any progress that I should make in the future. It was not a good experience for me but knowing my mother that was exactly what I expected to hear from her. She was, by nature, a most magnanimous human being and our relationship, particularly in the years prior to my leaving was flawless. In the end, a decision was made, I would set off on a journey full of uncertainties, leaving behind all those who were dear to me – all the things that I loved and cared for, this land that I so treasured. It was an emotional turmoil, which ranked above any that I can remember in my entire lifetime.

On the eve of leaving Guyana to join the S.S Venezuela to begin my sojourn to the other end of the world, I was overwhelmed with mixed emotions. Surrounded as I was by relatives, colleagues and well-wishers who had gathered to celebrate my departure and to wish me a successful journey truly aroused my sentimentality. It was an evening full of fun and laughter but it was also one when many things were said to me, most of it reminding me of the fullness and vibrancy of my youth, growing up as I did in a small village such as ours. I was reminded that I was the first of our family to venture so far afield. Until then it did not register fully in my consciousness and the fear of getting it wrong was very real. I was reminded how much I would miss my Mum's home cooking. Her culinary skills were amazing and since eating was one of the great joys of my life, I was in no doubt, if there was a downside to this grand venture of mine; it would have to be the absence of her wonderful meals. By far the highlight of the evening was to remind myself of how much I would miss the singing group that I was part of. We were called the Bachelors. We plied our harmonising skills – Fitzroy, Denis and myself – for four glorious years and became very well known especially among the ladies.

Our singing took us everywhere and as young men we harboured thoughts that it would staircase us to stardom. To say that we indulged in grand aspirations of making it big was putting it mildly. However, it was not long before we found out that the window of opportunity would never open for us. Nevertheless, the measure of success we enjoyed gave us much pleasure and engendered memories that cannot be erased.

As events went, this was an evening full of laughter and tears. One that was unequalled for its mixed emotions. It was important for me to be objective. I explained to everyone that my stay abroad would only be temporary and that soon I would be back in my own environment with my relatives and friends, just as it should be. Unfortunately, I knew not what destiny had in store for me.

My journey to Trinidad was quite an unusual one. When I arrived at Piarco Airport that late May afternoon, I was confident in my mind that the arrangements I had made beforehand were airtight and trouble free. Not one for taking risks, I expected my pal, Rudy Rolston who had spent many years in Guyana and was now residing in Trinidad, to be present on my arrival. As a matter of course, many of the passengers who were en route to England were hotel accommodated. Mine was a special arrangement and I was positive there would be no hitch in my plans.

I was experiencing flying for the first time in my life and not liking it one little bit. The 'Art Williams' as I recall was the only plane that flew to Trinidad. The plane had a double function. It combined its passenger activity with fetching meat from the savannah, which borders Brazil, and without a doubt, my trip across the ocean was marred by a strange and unpleasant whiff that confused my senses. Once the journey had begun and although the plane appeared clean, this noxious atmosphere within overwhelmed me. I arrived in Trinidad light headed and in a state of delirium and was only too pleased to remove myself from the environs of that plane.

I cleared immigration with the greatest of expectations hoping to see my friend once more for a happy reunion. But unfortunately he was nowhere to be seen and my expectations soon gave way to panic. Everyone that I had travelled with, including Élan, were now gone. All the passengers were picked up and taken to a hotel as part of the arrangement. I was left behind because of the private plan I had made with Rudy in Trinidad. The evening sun was quickly making way for nightfall. With my presence at the airport becoming more and more conspicuous, one thing was certain; my well-planned venture was beginning to collapse and my situation becoming desperate.

My arrangement obviously depended very much on being met and escorted into Port of Spain and what was now needed was a clear focus to get me out of my present predicament, it was then that good fortune struck. Rudy, who was a policeman both in Guyana and now Trinidad, was unable to make the airport journey as a result of work commitments. His attempt to make alternative plans also failed. After I had been waiting for two hours, a taxi driver approached me and asked if I needed help. Even though I told him that I was waiting for a friend, he insisted that going with him was the only sensible alternative. He collected my luggage and started towards his cab with me reluctantly in tow. My fear being he had an agenda all his own. My concern was that he seemed too willing to help but it was now pretty dark and there was no other choice available.

On our way to Port of Spain he spoke constantly and gave high praise to Dr Eric Williams' government. He was a patriot if ever I saw one. His robust chatter and his willingness to show off the achievements of his city calmed my fears and extinguished any notion I may have developed along the way. What was on offer was simply amazing. This stranger took me out of my misery and landed me in the safekeeping of my friend's home without any due reward.

Regaining my composure subsequently and remembering that episode, something struck me as remarkable. At no time did I offer him payment for the journey, but more importantly and to the best of my knowledge, he did not ask for any. It was simply an act of kindness that perhaps comes your way once in a lifetime. As for my friend Rudy, he was relieved and overjoyed that I was able to make the journey safely.

Every now and then I still remember that act of kindness. It ranks highly in my estimation, especially from someone who was a total and complete stranger; it was also a good omen for me at the start of my travel. If ever guardian angels exist, I found mine at Piarco Airport.

MY JOURNEY TO ENGLAND

My journey started in the middle of May 1959, arriving in Trinidad to join the Italian liner, SS Venezuela. It was a totally new experience. I was filled with nervous excitement and apprehension, both in equal measure. I was by nature, a home-grown boy. My sense of adventure was limited to playing a game of cricket in the afternoons and meeting up with the lads in the evenings after supper. To embark on a journey to the other end of the world was extremely out of character and although I was truly on my way, I kept wondering whether the decision to leave was in fact the right one.

My friend Elan was not without his own problems, he decided to get married one week before departure, and that in my experience was a very brave act. In many ways his presence and the encouragement he was able to give helped to calm my own anxieties.

The first evening on the ship was far and away a most unpleasant experience as I recall. The sea was very choppy and the liner, large as it was, rocked a little unsteadily. Throughout the night, I endured an awful, queasy sensation, so when I was summoned to breakfast the following morning, I simply had no enthusiasm or desire for food.

That morning and throughout the entire day at mealtime, Elan and I found dissatisfaction with the way we were treated. Crammed in a corner of the restaurant, on long tables and treated in an extraordinary ill-mannered way did not please us in the least. Equally upsetting was the behaviour of some of the folks around those tables. There were people from every Island in the Caribbean and it was a case – or so it seemed to us – of every man for himself. Grabbing things, shouting and the general misconduct left a great deal to be desired. The servers, perhaps because of the language difficulties, reacted in a rude and arrogant manner which, ultimately, caused unnecessary friction. To live in an environment like that for another three weeks was not what my colleague and I had envisaged. Elan was determined that the following day things would be different. What ever it was, I kept hoping that it was not confrontational because I was sure I had no appetite for it.

The morning after, Elan beckoned to me to follow him to a different seating arrangement. They were two people sitting at a table for four and we decided to fill the vacant seats. I instinctively knew that the action we took would carry with it its own difficulties. The fact that the people there did not seem to approve of us merely compounded the problem. After some moments of waiting, I realised that my instinct was spot on. The steward, having seen us in our new environment, came over looking most agitated. "Why are you sitting here? You have allocation over there", he said, pointing to the long tables. "You not get served here," he said. "You go to your allocation".

Elan was enraged. He quickly got to his feet. "I've paid good money for this journey – and I expect to be treated properly. I shall not be going back to that cattle market. I'm staying here and that is final". Elan was positively looking at the steward straight in his eyes. For a moment they eyeballed each other, no quarter given.

"OK" said the steward, "I see that you get moved". He turned and disappeared. The silence was deafening. This, for me, was a most fearful moment. A choice had to be made. I would have to be loyal and give Elan my support or retreat back to the relative safety of the long tables. The idea of defiance did not appeal to me but running away would certainly not solve the problem. So we waited.

It was then that I made an observation, which was somewhat significant. For the first time I realised that the attitude towards us was far from healthy. The mood and general friendliness that was in evidence in the areas where other people were sitting, mainly whites, was in stark contrast to where we were and my mood changed very rapidly from fear to annoyance. It was not that we were craving respect; it was merely that it would appear that there was a preconceived plan to treat one set of people different from the rest. That was an invaluable lesson, especially for my consciousness and it has served me in good stead ever since.

The chief steward was a tall and elegant man. For some strange reason he seemed to have a smile on his face. His command of English was excellent, and his manner somewhat graceful. He enquired politely why we had moved and we informed him that we were unhappy with conditions on the long tables. He made it known that there were rules to be followed and that we would make everyone's job easier if we were to adhere to them. We acknowledged the difficulty but stressed the importance of wanting to be comfortable for the rest of the journey. For a while he hesitated, then, calling his junior steward aside, he carried on a brief but animated discussion before returning to us. "Gentlemen" he said, "My job is hard enough without difficulties from you two – but I have made a decision. Providing you two are prepared to remain at this table for the rest of the trip, you can stay".

We agreed and thanked him. He turned to his junior steward and spoke in Italian. Whatever he said did not seem to please the man. Perhaps he felt betrayed by his senior officer. The response however was brief. The chief steward, still smiling broadly, placed his arm around the young man's shoulder and in a consoling manner took him away.

For one, I felt triumphant. It was a small victory, not only for me but also for Elan. His courage had won the day but I knew that it would have come to nothing without my support.

Throughout that entire journey, I thought of that chief steward. His image as a kind and understanding person had taken favour with me. He was the one person I was ready to speak of and give conscious respect to whenever I saw him. Why did I so greatly admire him? It's difficult to say – after all it was only a small act of kindness he performed – a bit of charity, a damage limitation exercise, nothing more. Maybe I was impressed with the skill and confidence with which it was done, skills that he must have acquired over the years functioning in that capacity. The lesson learnt from that incident travelled with me for many years. Highlighting perhaps what developed countries would do to their less fortunate neighbours; offering a bit of charity here or there to make them feel good. They use a system so tried and tested, so honed and nurtured over many, many years, that developing countries fail to notice that all they are getting is high class diplomacy and a bit of charity.

As a young man growing up, I have always heard of the potential of Guyana; its mineral resources are vast and in the course of time we would all benefit from it. Today even with the resources intact, we are now regarded as one of the poorest countries in the world. The promise to develop Guyana remains just that.

Because of a strike somewhere along the way to England, we were forced to change route, which to our displeasure kept us on the liner longer than we wanted to be. Although, there were those who took great delight in the extended time given; if only to satisfy their newfound relationships. Some of the women found it difficult to resist the advances of those amorous men and consequently fell victims to love, which was not meant to last. The more adventurous ones simply accepted what was on offer without a care for the people they were coming to meet. Consequently they were a few cases where ladies transferred their love and loyalty in mid ocean to men they just met with nothing but misery and heartache for those that were waiting for them at the other end.

My friend Elan had his own woes. Only just married, he was homesick and missing his newly wed wife. For me, I was full of nervous contemplation. I was determined to stand resolutely to my original plan. Simply to work hard, finish my course, travel to America for practical workshop experience and return to Guyana within five to ten years.

The journey, which seemed an eternity, further extended because of the strike; nevertheless it afforded us the opportunity of seeing places that were not originally on the agenda. The places that were of particular interest to me were Barcelona and Tenerife. Both were exciting and scenic but the one that had me spellbound both for its fascination and shear delight was Cannes. We disembarked that evening and were fascinated by the colour and lights that cascaded around us. It came to our notice that this was the place where the rich and successful came out to play, where film stars assembled. The yachts and hotels all lit up – radiated splendour such as I have never seen. It was breathtakingly beautiful – a true visual feast of colours.

Undoubtedly, these were all magnificent places and hardly surprising they represented the personification of what I expected Europe to be like. Quite apart from its beauty, charm and economic advancement, there was a degree of prosperity that was hardly in evidence in countries such as ours. The heightened standard of existence, which this showed, was in stark contrast to places such as Guyana. It was not difficult to observe also, unlike poor countries, very little trace of poverty. Without a doubt, the contrast was a sobering experience.

Cannes was the last port of call. My journey on the S.S. Venezuela had finally come to an end. It was a long and tiresome voyage and being of a restless nature, the crossing tested my patience to the fullest. Three weeks of travel in my opinion could have been spent in a more rewarding way. One reason was due to sharing a cabin with people whose habits and mannerisms were not compatible with mine. Menus that were repetitive and not often tastefully prepared, was another factor. Passengers, the vast majority who did not communicate in English, or in any other way for that matter, contributed nothing to the general atmosphere of the journey. Importantly also, was the gulf that existed between the well-heeled ones who were having the time of their lives with their cocktails and other sophisticated mixes and ourselves, the 'them and us' scenario, left me with no pleasant memory of that long voyage. It may be correct in saying, since it was some time ago, that apart from the few folk – Gladstone Austin being one of them – that kept our interest alive on that vessel, the voyage for me anyway was very ordinary.

However my focus by now was totally in another direction. I was full on my own anxieties of what I was about to experience in the United Kingdom. George Boucher, my ex-school mate and friend, who was eagerly expecting my imminent arrival, told me by correspondence of some of the places of interest that made London such an exciting city. Places that I was eager to behold for myself, such as the Houses of Parliament, Trafalgar Square, Piccadilly Circus-West End, trains that run underground, Marylebone Cricket Club-Lords, and of course the Oval. My expectation was overwhelmed by all this, as a result my focus was simply more getting to England above all else. However, it is worth mentioning a situation, if only for its humour and which went a long way in raising not to mention a degree of happiness to many of the lads on board. It still brings a smile to my face whenever I recall it and it's all to do with wine.

Each day we were given an ample supply of wine, especially with our midday meal. Unfortunately it was almost always rejected, primarily because it was dry wine which apparently many of the lads did not appreciate. This situation lasted for a week and a half.

Then someone had a brainstorm and came up with a brilliant idea of adding sugar to it, renaming it 'wet wine' as opposed to its dry contemporary and that had much to do with the remarkable change that was in evidence. The generous smiles and exaggerated gestures was proof that the new brew was making a solid mark on the lads and what was more, they were loving it!

Our stay in Cannes was brief. We waited in an enclosure for our train journey out – and it was surprising to see the interest we created. We were something of a spectacle. People were peering through the wire mesh at us as though we were in a zoo. Perhaps it was merely curiosity at seeing so many black folks in one place.

The journey through Europe by train can only be described as arduous. It was lacking in proper management and as a result, little was given to us by way of food. The train was full to capacity and those of us that were fortunate to find seating were not very charitable in sharing. In the circumstances, many were made to do the entire journey standing up. It was for all of us a major test of stamina and resilience. By the time we arrived at Dieppe, I was seriously questioning the wisdom of this venture. I was by nature very slim but fit, so it was hardly surprising that by the time we arrived at Newhaven, after experiencing what I would regard as a totally unfriendly crossing, there was very little of me left. The rough seas certainly did not do us many favours and for a while I told myself that if I did not see another boat or train in my lifetime, I would not worry unduly. However, I was truly buoyed by the fact that at long last we had arrived at a British port. Travelling as we did for three weeks on an Italian liner, and across Europe listening to unfamiliar languages; depressed me tremendously. Hearing the spoken word again made me feel very much at home. The journey was almost at an end except for one more train ride to London.

We arrived at Victoria station on June 15th. It was early evening and the sun was shining brightly. It was unusual to see so many people in one place, let alone a railway station. I felt a tinge of excitement but that soon gave way to fear. With such a crowd it would be quite easy to miss my friend and old school mate, George Boucher, whose accommodation and guidance I could not have done without, in those early months of my arrival. Missing him would have left me with no other option but to find Finsbury Park, grip (suitcase) and all, on my own. Quite frankly, I did not fancy my chances of negotiating that journey successfully. My worry was totally misplaced because as I came out I saw the unmistakable face of George, waving frantically at me. My relief was total; at least I had a friend in London that I could depend on.

George was accompanied by a friend who chatted relentlessly to him. That suited me no end as it gave me the opportunity to observe this larger than life city and to try to regain some composure after such a tiring journey.

To be honest, that breathless expectancy and nervous anticipation was now extinguished. Seeing George in the flesh gave me all the assurance I needed. I was now in safe hands but even in that emotional state I could not help observing how sombre – even to a point of blandness – the dress mode of the inhabitants were. Everything seemed so grey and colourless, which naturally gave me the impression that folks were either coming from or going to a funeral. No wonder my attire – a fawn suit – commanded conspicuous attention. What was also noticeable was the pace everyone seemed to be setting. This helter-skelter habit was in stark contrast to what I was accustomed. Given that there was no fire - why the haste? Of course it was not long before I realised that every minute counts in a large metropolis such as this. Indeed time was perhaps the most important asset in the general life style of this city. I could hardly fail to notice also, the joined up houses with chimneys. They seemed so novel to me and quite a departure from homes in the tropics. I cannot say with hand on heart that I was immediately impressed with my new environment but there was no denying the fact – something that impacted on me immediately – that I was now in the presence of a society that was properly developed and well structured. Evidence of this power and might was in great abundance. It was then that I finally realised the amazing difference between countries that have and those that have not. It was a chilling and somewhat frightening experience and instinctively I knew that my village attitude would not fit adequately in this new environment. It was therefore imperative that I made the necessary adjustment to suit this new place. One thing was certain now; there was no turning back.

The bus was almost full but the couple behind me concerned me most. They were in deep conversation and seemingly enjoying it. To me it was some kind of dialect that baffled me. My constant glances drew the attention of George. He looked at me and smiled. Still puzzled I smiled back. "Soon you'll be speaking like that – it's what you call cockney". That was pretty ironic to me. The average Londoner indulges in a dialect, which seemed indigenous to the area, universally used and by no stretch of the imagination could be considered proper spoken English. It was not the kind that I listened to on the BBC Radio back in my native Guyana. I expected to hear this from every English person, to have the experience not many hours ago, of immigration complaining bitterly about not understanding what these people (Blacks) were saying seems strange indeed. How on earth were they able to understand cockney?

My destination was 23A Woodstock Road; a backroom which I shared with George for almost a year. My journey was now truly over and as I set my grip down and looked through the window, I was confronted with the spectacle of a British Rail yard. Having not long seen Cannes at its best, this site could hardly be anything but depressing.

LIFE IN LONDON:
MY FIRST EXPERIENCE

The following morning George gave me a key to the front door, offered some advice and was off to work. My first night in London was not a comfortable one. The trains, passing with annoying regularity, interrupted my rest; however, the day was fine and I was determined to go out for a stroll. It seemed a better idea than watching men wash train windows. As I reached Finsbury Park Station, I saw a shabby looking person coming towards me. I was warned to be careful by my ex-boss, Mr Sunderland, an Englishman whose opinions I valued a great deal, so my first instinct was to give him a wide berth. He beckoned to me and since he seemed harmless enough, I hesitated. "Please mate could you give me the price of a cup of tea?" he asked. He looked dreadful and it was truly unfortunate that I was unable to help since I had no English currency. It was significant to me since it was the first time I had seen a European beggar. The Europeans I knew back in my country were always in charge – riding horses and living in fabulous homes. The films we saw always portrayed whites as rich, powerful and successful human beings. Never would I have thought a white beggar would confront me on my first day on a London street. It was indeed a culture shock.

The entire experience; moving from a small village with a distinct but small communal environment to a large metropolis, impacted instantaneously on me. The environment that I came from was easy paced – friendly and engaging. Everyone knew everyone as a norm and without thought, we related to each other. "Good morning" – "Hello" - "Good Afternoon" – "Good evening" was a taken-for- granted form of behaviour.

I lived in a house with many rooms and the 'space factor' was never a problem. On arrival here I readily observed that interaction between people; especially on the streets, was a definite 'no no'. Stranger still was speaking to people, even those that you worked with, and getting little or no response whatsoever. I mentioned the oddity to George who found my remarks amusing.

"You are not in Guyana now, mate" he joked, "This is England. No one has time to be friendly – so change your ways". I found that good advice and tried to refrain from doing so but old habits diehard and it was some time before I was able to adjust to a more realistic way.

The room I shared with George was of average proportions. Having been here in his sister's house for over two years, his room was well equipped. We shared the kitchen with other tenants. However, that posed no problem as I hardly saw them anyway. Be that as it may, the element of being confined to one room with washing facilities down in the basement proved a major inconvenience. The general idea of washing, especially in the winter months, became an extremely tricky endeavour.

My friend Elan was far less fortunate than I was. I discovered that he lived a mere stone's throw away from Finsbury Park. His location was Highbury Barn. My first visit to his residence shocked me enormously. It was a very large room, something of a dormitory existence – five beds, a congested kitchen and one toilet. Those were the amenities that were available. The two paraffin heaters were never adequate enough to warm the oversized room. The paraffin heater, being an important feature in the long cold winter months of those early years, became multi-purpose in their use as a secondary stove. The traffic in the kitchen, especially in the evenings became so acute that the appliance was often used to boil kettles, among other uses, mainly for quick results and to alleviate the pressure of the kitchen. Friendly as the 'lamp' (as it was commonly called) was, misuse of it very often caused serious injury and even death by fire. However, conditions were desperate and very often desperate situations produce desperate measures.

Routinely, Elan, some other friends and I would find ourselves in the Highbury Barn, a pub across the way. Looking back, I wonder, in order of importance, what was the motivation for so doing. Was it the beer? Which was 'affordable'; was it the atmosphere or simply a place to keep warm? If the truth is to be told, there was merit in all of them.

Interestingly, the Spartan existence of those lads never culled their high spirits and bounding enthusiasm for life. It was always a pleasure to be among them. Their humour and wit was all-prevailing. It was nevertheless, a period when many of us were exploited in a most awful way. Landlords grew rich on the backs of many of us. That we were able to extricate ourselves from the misery so many of us had experienced, was in itself, a tremendous achievement on its own. Fortunately for people like myself, I have survived those years and still retain enough grey matter to recall them.

EARNING A LIVING IN LONDON

George was a postal worker and he advised that I try for a job with London Transport. The Post Office needed references at that time and since that was a long process taking months, it was hardly worth pursuing. Transport was the better option and anyway it was warmer in the winter months.

We arrived at Baker Street early that Tuesday morning and I was fortunate to be one of the first to be interviewed. I did not know what to expect, being only five days in the country. George informed me that after the initial interview I would be escorted to the door by the officer and told to try some other time. He indicated that it was hardly possible to get the job on my first visit. I was prepared for that and as I was escorted out I began making my way to the exit door. The officer asked me where I was going. I stood there, totally perplexed, not knowing what to say.

"I give the orders here young man – now follow me please" he said. I was given a test – another interview, a medical examination and was told that my training would commence at Lambeth North the following Monday.

George was far from pleased to see me several hours later. Time was pressing on for him to be at work. Aware of the fact that I would not know where to turn, he was forced to wait. I came out smiling.

"What kept you all this time?" he asked, looking at his watch. "I've got the job. I start on Monday," I announced.

George almost collapsed with surprise and shock. "You did what?" He enquired.

"I start training on Monday," I repeated.

He stood there staring at me in utter disbelief. "I have been in this country over two years; tried four times for a job in London Transport and you just came here, and in less than a week and got it?"

"I am afraid so," I said.

"You know something – there is no bloody justice in this world" I laughed as I watched my friend's reaction. He was not annoyed because I got the job. He was a good friend. George was simply bemused and surprised at my immediate success, especially since his own attempts had failed on numerous occasions.

My first posting after my training began at Holborn Station under a station master by the name of Ellis. He was an ex-army sergeant - stern and very particular but under that exterior he appeared quite decent. It would not be out of place to say the expression he wore which was very serious, frightened the life out of me – initially anyway. Perhaps because it was the first time I was working with Europeans which principally was a novel experience or perhaps, more to the point I was still carrying all the baggage of my recent past – which gave me the impression that white people must not only be respected but feared. What was a bonus for me in many ways was that the foreman, Don Brown, was a Caribbean man. Don was both friendly and outgoing. His advice and subsequent openness benefited me enormously. It helped me to acquire inner strength and a measure of confidence. Another staff member who helped me greatly was Joyce Duncan, like me, a Guyanese. Her positive attitude was good for me and we developed a friendship that has lasted to this day.

My first assignment was to be attached to an elderly but affable Englishman named Stan. Our task was to wash and repair the white lines on the platform. Stan laughed easily and asked a lot of questions – like "why did you come to this Country?" - a question that was asked on numerous occasions since. If I were to be given ten pence for every time I've answered it I would have been fairly well off indeed. Before we started he took out his cigarettes and offered me one. Out of politeness rather than need, I took it, since it was not a habit in which I ever indulged. The following day – still assigned to Stan, he decided to have a cigarette, this time one was not on offer. He looked up and blew the smoke into the air, looked at me and smiled.

"Sorry mate," said Stan. "I can't offer you a fag today; you never gave me back the one I gave you yesterday". I was utterly bemused; firstly, the word 'fag' was totally new to me but more importantly, I did not think it necessary to reciprocate. After all, it was only a cigarette. Later that evening I discussed the matter with Joyce who told me about the new custom; that the normal practice in England is not to take without giving back. I immediately responded by buying a packet of cigarettes and offering it to Stan. He declined politely, accepting only the one he gave me. I was now becoming aware of the customs and habits of this new land. Far from the one I left behind.

The second week at Holborn was simply unforgettable. It was a week when I was given a duty, which seemed totally ridiculous. Here was I only a few short weeks in the Country with little knowledge of the geography or anything else of London and was placed on a strategic duty directing traffic. The sheer volume of people overwhelmed me. To say I was both confused and petrified after the first fifteen minutes would be a total understatement. What I could not fail to observe – even in my distressed state however, was the pace of the commuters moving helter-skelter in every direction. The questions were not only many, they were thick and fast. 'How do I get to one station or another'; 'where do I change?' 'How long does it take to get from A to B', etc, etc.

To say that I coped with any the questions adequately, would be a misrepresentation of the truth and what should have been an hour and a half seemed like an eternity. I developed very quickly what I felt was a ploy to combat this relentless barrage of questions. For most of the time, I pointed in one direction or another and for most of the time, people were far too busy to waste their time with someone who looked more like a frightened child lost in a large crowd.

One very elegant passenger returned. I recall giving him information that was obviously not correct. As he got closer, I realised he was about to query my knowledge about the destination he was seeking. It was not surprising that I did my best to pretend that I was unaware of his presence. He appeared not to be angry but neither was he amused.

"Young man, you sent me on the Central Line and I really wanted the Piccadilly". He looked at me pointedly, "I get the impression you don't know what you're doing". He declared.

I found myself nodding in the affirmative. After all, what was the point of lying?

"Well!" he said, "If this job is going to be yours for any length of time, I would, if I were you, try to understand what it is all about and stop giving the impression of an animated goldfish in an oversized fish pond."

He did not wait for an answer and as I watched him go I quite realised that it would be the longest week on record to cope with; and it was; although through diligent effort I was able to perform appreciably better in later days.

That particular duty I avoided like the plague and did my best to rid myself of it. Interestingly enough and by coincidence, I was privileged to observe a work mate of mine performing that very duty. His knowledge, efficiency and confidence amazed me. It was as if he had done that duty all his life and I wondered if I would ever be able to master the art of knowing places in the same way as my colleague did.

On arrival home, I indicated to George of the marvellous way Harry conducted himself and the knowledge he was capable of. George reassured me that Harry was no genius. He was a mere mortal who worked long enough at the station to have acquired full knowledge of places and it would not be long before I am able to have expertise equal to him about the job. I wanted to believe him but just then it seemed an impossible task to attain.

Six months on, I began reflecting on what George had said and he was right. After all, I had only been in the Country a few weeks and in the job even less. The knowledge in terms of understanding more about places and things became almost automatic, which was a pity because Harry was not as much a genius as I once thought.

Those six months were mostly spent on the Central Line, with Holborn as my home base. Those were months that gave me an insight of different places and working methods that was instrumental in obtaining knowledge and building self-confidence.

My stay as a station man at Holborn was a relatively short one. Ten months into the job I was encouraged by a young English foreman who did rest days there, to apply for a new position. The job advertised was for foreman ticket collectors. Mike was a pleasant and very helpful person. We got on well together and I found his advice on matters relating to the job most helpful. It was also the time when I was in the process of sending for my then girlfriend, Gloria (who has been my wife for the last forty years), with a view to marriage. With the extra cash that I could earn as a foreman, it would no doubt be a big financial boost that would be of tremendous advantage to me. The only problem was, I was in the Country less than a year – knew nothing about the business of running or managing stations outside of sweeping platforms or washing tiles. This step up seemed too steep an elevation for my comfort. This was where Mike came in. He showed great patience in explaining the task that I was about to undertake and expressed enough confidence in my ability to do the job as a foreman, adequately. That being the case it was not long before I decided. It occurred to me however, that the friendship between Mike and I seemed strangely odd. I was being observed in a quizzical way. Members of the staff would give me wry looks and somehow along the way I felt it a duty to ask why.

The opportunity came one evening when Stan and I were the only two people in the mess room. I enquired why so many members of staff seemed reluctant to engage Mike in meaningful conversation. Stan for a moment looked puzzled then he burst out laughing.

"You mean you don't know?" He enquired.

"No I have no idea" I retorted innocently.

"The guy is as queer as a coot ... I thought you knew".

It took a while to sink in. To me, he was no more than a decent person. All my dealings with him suggested only the fact that he was a kind hearted and honest person. He showed me no indication of being different and since his general demeanour was strictly above board, respect for the man was perfectly in order. A person's sexuality is not the concern of any one else and should be viewed broadly that way. To be gay in the sixties was considered taboo by much of society. My! How times have changed.

My three weeks training to become a foreman ticket inspector was very intense. My self-confidence was low and that ultimately affected my enthusiasm. There were many aspects of railway work to learn in those short weeks and the instructors at Lambeth were thorough and very serious men. Their expectations were high and much effort was needed in order to succeed. The three weeks seemed like months. To know about rules and regulations, lifts and escalators, signals, booking office and cabin work, was simply not easy for someone like me whose knowledge of such things was totally limited. In the end though, my determination to succeed won through and so in early autumn of 1960 I finally became a foreman.

Three Caribbean men emerged as relief foremen and were immediately under the cosh. How could three black guys - with no seniority be relief foreman? The answer was simple – the position was new and since those who were senior to us did not apply, we obviously got it. Nevertheless, it created a large degree of resentment up and down the Northern Line.

The first year was by far the worst. My lack of knowledge for trains and for the geography of London set me at a distinct disadvantage. If that were my only worry it would have been comparatively easy. The fact that I had to learn different facets of the job, against staff that were not always co-operative, was totally another matter. Some were downright awkward. We were given keys for the purpose of opening stations with bunches so huge that they became burdensome. Knowing the relevant ones for stations that we worked at became an important part of the job. That way we were able to leave the rest behind. It also became important for me to check out stations in advance in order for me to get an idea of what I had to deal with. Even then it was not always easy to get information which assisted me in getting the job done. For a time it became very stressful.

There were three of us, Davis, Lewis and myself. Davis was short, dark and stocky. He was also the oldest of us three. He never settled on the job and within months he was demoted because of his inability to grasp things quickly and he eventually left the job. Lewis and I were younger and more resilient but nevertheless we were under severe pressure. Being a foreman on a station where there was no one to talk to, can be a lonely occupation indeed. There were many such days and more often than not my only friend and companion was a book.

During the early period at Camden Town, we were directly under a station master (S.M.) by the name of Crooks. Although he was one of many, he was the senior S.M.

It was also the era when all black people looked alike. Lewis was six foot one inch tall, round face, broad shoulders, I was five foot nine, a small face and generally skinny; yet the white staff there found it difficult to distinguish one from the other. The throwaway statement was always; "How can we tell you apart – all you people look alike". Initially I tried explaining the differences but to no avail. It was that period when white folks were governed by a certain 'mind set' of which they undoubtedly became a prisoner.

It was also the time when 'No coloureds, no Irish and no dogs' prevailed. Times were certainly not easy for us. Finding suitable accommodation was anything but easy. My girlfriend's arrival was imminent and finding proper lodgings were my main objective. Thoughts of leaving 23 Woodstock Road played on my mind. It was a good place to live and I was fortunate to have been there, especially considering the sub-standard conditions that some of my colleagues have had to endure. Living four and sometimes five to one room was not out of the ordinary. When George got married and moved to the room adjacent to mine, I had the freedom to accommodate some of my friends who arrived in England subsequently. One such person was Fitzroy who assisted me in choosing my first radiogram, an 'Ultra'. It was a beautiful piece of furniture that gave me many wonderful moments of pleasure and now although it is nothing more than a relic; it is still in my possession. Its purpose is purely sentimental.

The one moment that stands out as perhaps the bleakest in England - was in that room on Christmas Day 1959. George who was related to the Barnwell's, spent most of the day with them downstairs. I was invited to do the same but declined. I felt it would have been an intrusion; since I was new there and not fully acquainted with the family, I decided to stay away.

That morning I stood and stared through the window for what must have been ages. It was so very, very quiet. Nothing stirred. Since I did not know what to expect, the question I kept asking myself was; is this what Christmas Day is in England? Surrounded by four walls, a paraffin lamp to keep me warm and a window that looks out onto a drab railway yard? My mind swiftly reflected back to Plaisance, to my mum's home cooking. Her pepper pot and garlic pork, her fine cakes and home-made wine, to my friends and family back there, to an environment that was bright and cheerful, with happiness exuding from every corner on this wonderful day and wondered if the sacrifice I made in leaving would ever be justified. One thing was certain, if ever I was to experience another Christmas in England, I would carry a different status – that of a married man.

LOOKING FOR ACCOMMODATION AND GETTING MARRIED

My search for an adequate place became very problematic. The exclusive use of 'No coloureds, no Irish and no dogs' deterred any possible or successful attempt to acquire worthwhile accommodation. Overhearing my plight, an English workmate advanced some information that gave me nothing but joy. She told me of an English friend, someone she knew very well who had a flat to rent that would best suit my needs. Assuring me that her friend was not the type to turn me down, I was in quick pursuit to avail myself of this unexpected opportunity. The landlady was very pleasant. We spoke for a while on the phone about the suitability of the flat. She did not ask what my nationality was and I got the distinct impression as my co-worker suggested that she had an open mind.

With high hopes of getting the flat I needed, I set off for Stamford Hill, a short journey. Arriving there I rang the bell and a woman approached. She opened the door and for a while looked shocked. Her cautious manner gave me the impression that she had not paid enough attention to my dialect – perhaps thinking I was English. I told her that I had spoken to her ten minutes earlier with regard to the accommodation. Forcing what seemed like a smile she informed me that the flat was gone. She was far from convincing but rallied quickly when the landlord arrived. He showed no emotion what so ever, explaining very quickly but firmly that the flat was not available. Before I could respond, the door was slammed shut. This unceremonious behaviour left me shattered. It is an extraordinary low feeling when you actually experience rejection of such nature. Rejection based simply on the colour of your skin. What was remarkable about that era was the fact that the British, who are always considered animal lovers, were quite deliberate in including dogs as an exemption to their homes as if Blacks and Irish were not enough.

I was explaining the incident to someone at Warren Street when an Antiguan friend, Greta, told me to look no further. There was a flat where she lived and she was positive I would get it. The reason being, most of the people living there were Caribbean and Mr Martin, the landlord gave preference to us. She was absolutely correct. His rent was slightly higher than the norm but it was a price worth paying if only for peace of mind. He was by comparison to landlords of that era, a reasonable man. I had the unfortunate experience of meeting such a landlord in Turnham Green. It was where Gloria stayed briefly. He was a Mr Price, an arrogant, obtrusive man, who felt we should be forever grateful to live in his house, unpleasant and sub-standard as it was. Mr Martin was not such a man. He was by and large, almost invisible. He treated his tenants with respect and more often than not, the only knowledge of his presence on the premises was his cigar smoke which he invariably left behind, long after he was gone.

With Gloria having arrived in August of 1960, the date for our wedding was set for 15th October of that year. The distance between us – her living in Turnham Green with relatives, was most inconvenient. Being on shift work and hardly knowing what I would be doing from week to week did not help the situation one tiny bit. Unable to communicate with her since a phone was not available, caused my proposed marriage – small as it was, to take on an extraordinary twist. In fact, it was sheer theatre. That Friday I arrived at Turnham Green expecting everything to be normal, only to find that the consent form which should have been sent to the registrar days ago did not happen. To my astonishment the form was still in Gloria's custody.

The rules were breached. That being the case our marriage was off. What was I supposed to do? After all the hard work I had put in, things were not going as planned. I hurried down to the registrar's office, minutes before closing time, in the forlorn hope of getting the registrar to change her mind; to no avail. Rules are made to be followed and that was that. All my pleas fell on deaf ears. Suddenly an idea developed; should I get married on the following day, would she be prepared to accommodate me by coming? At first she rejected the idea right out of hand. The Church would not allow it – and Sundays was totally outside of business hours. At that point I felt the world was coming down on my not particularly broad shoulders. Much was at stake; the holidays which I had managed to squeeze from London Transport for this occasion, the general preparation for the event and the total disappointment of friends and relatives. With all that in mind, I persisted. Much of it was invention, fabrication and embellishment. Eventually I got from her a positive response. She made me a promise. Provided that the church was prepared to marry me on a Sunday, she would, as a personal favour to me, make herself available. What I saw in her eyes was pity but that was not my immediate concern.

The giant task was still to be performed; getting the Roman Catholic Church to agree to do the same. I scurried back to Chiswick not only to inform the priest (Father Johnson) that I could not be married on the planned day due to the unfortunate incident with the registrar but to ask him to perform the very difficult task of marrying me on the Sunday. Father Johnson was sympathetic but firm - it could not be done. The church had put in place a great deal of work to accommodate a Saturday wedding which unfortunately had to be scrapped. Apart from that, it was not normal practice to do so. The church's schedule simply did not permit it. Armed with the knowledge that the registrar was willing to break with tradition, I pressed on. My circumstances demanded that I got married on the Sunday. I explained to him that the holiday I extracted from work was a short one – one week. I was getting new furnishings for the flat on the Monday. That apart, there were numerous things to be done to accommodate my new bride but most essentially, I needed some time to be with her.

Father Johnson decided after what seemed like an eternity of pleading and beseeching, to give ground. He decided as a matter of goodwill to marry us. I had triumphed at long last.

Returning to Finsbury Park that Friday evening, I was both mentally and physically tired and wondered if there was any other problem lurking around the corner and if so, was I able to withstand it. As sure as 'God made little green apples'; there were. That Saturday morning Christopher brought me my wedding cake with the bad news that the official bridesmaid (Gloria's cousin), had decided, for reasons best known to herself that she would not be attending the wedding. That meant another journey to Turnham Green, this time to ask another cousin to fill the vacancy. Doreen was not unfavourable to the idea; it was just that she was totally unprepared for the task. However, she obliged, so ending two days of absolute turmoil, unsurpassed by anything that has happened in my life since. Looking back, I can say the dividends paid for that experience, was that I grew up quickly from boy to man.

That Saturday evening I was determined to make it an unforgettable one. It was the last night of bachelorhood and the not so many friends were there to celebrate with me. Gloria and her contingent arrived and we were just getting into the swing of things when her uncle announced that he was taking the bride and the rest of her party back to Chiswick, wrecking what should have been a memorable night. After all the frustration of the last days, this was by comparison, a 'blip' but it was something I could have done without. With them gone, the few friends that were left did their best to drown their sorrows and hoped that the wedding day would be hitch free. Christopher Streaker, my very good friend, would remember that evening for another reason. Before midnight he was completely inebriated, an experience I would never allow him to forget.

Finally on the 16th October at 3.30 pm, after all that went before, Gloria Gordon became my wife, at Our Lady of Grace, St. Edwards Church, High Road Chiswick.

We moved into 8 Oakfield Road, Finsbury Park, on the day of our marriage and found it to be an interesting place. Our room was of average size with a kitchen that suffered from severe condensation, but it was ours exclusively and that made a wealth of difference. The house itself was fairly large and what was note worthy about it was the atmosphere that emanated from within those walls. Eight families lived there – one departed subsequently leaving seven – with the minimum of facilities. There was one bathroom that was coin operated and one toilet. Yet somehow, there was never any serious acrimony or disagreement. We managed in the best way possible and even in that modest condition, there was a fusion of friendship that was simply outstanding throughout our stay there. I still remember Oakfield Road with the fondest of memories.

REFLECTIONS

My formative years in London were filled with a great degree of uncertainty and being engulfed in a city as large as this, with all its complications, it created a measure of stress all of its own. This was an environment that in many ways contrasted with my accustomed norm. The long winter months, the wearing of winter gear, the indifference which was part and parcel of being a stranger (immigrant) in this huge metropolis, made London a lonely place for me. The period of adjustment was not easy to establish. It was therefore imperative, especially in those early months working with the underground to make acquaintances and forge friendships from a wide variety of new people from both continental Africa and the Caribbean. In many ways it became an interesting and very exciting period of our lives, as it gave us an opportunity to relate to each other in ways that would not have been possible otherwise. To that end, it was as refreshing as it was worthwhile, since friendships were formed that stood the test of time. It was the period in our lives that the weekend became an integral part of our existence. Meeting people was strictly a weekend affair, since we were preoccupied during the week with the task of earning a living. A friend once remarked that London was not a place for fun. It was an 'oversized workshop' and since most of us had a vision in mind or an ambition to fulfil, earning a living became an essential priority.

Forced by the prevailing circumstances around us, we did the best we could to engender a sense of satisfaction and light relief by meeting in each other's rooms, enjoying each other's company and making light, much of what we did over those long working periods. Sharing common interests, bonding and doing what comes naturally. It became a valid and most important part of our very existence. For many it became the most 'look forward to' time in the week. Much fun and enthusiasm was derived from our activities, such as drinking ginger wine, Stingo, Taragona, VP wine and listening to Ska. Enjoying Nat 'King' Cole, Brook Benton and others and generally reminiscing on things past and whatever came to mind. That much needed social recreation got us into conflict with both the British public and the press. We were called, noisy blacks, troublesome wogs, disruptive immigrants, disorderly folks with no regard for the community and much more.

Our main dilemma was the problematic task of reaching our colleagues and friends wherever they were. We were living great distances apart and traversing around the city was a logistic nightmare. In those days London ceased to exist after midnight. Taxi cabs (for who could afford them) hardly accommodated us and the way home after missing the last trains, was on foot. Very often, forced by these circumstances, we had no alternative than to remain where we were, even if it meant sleeping rough or no sleep at all until morning. For that reason, parties lasted longer than they should. Being young and resilient, that hardly mattered; although there were times when we were forced to attend work immediately after, without rest.

Many of the gatherings I attended were subject to some form of police presence, complaining of excessive noise or disturbances of one kind or another, very often without justification. It became clear in our minds that we were targeted. Of course there were those who blighted our prospects with an element of selfishness and total disregard for others by their actions – lacking consciousness and forgetting that we owed a duty to ourselves to respect the society we lived in. Unfortunately, that is 'the nature of the beast' for those who are oblivious of proper behaviour and therefore unable to function adequately within the realms of decency. However, I would be interested to hear of any society on Earth that is void of such social misfits.

The initial years of my marriage were not entirely without friction, since being young, restless and having friends that were bachelors, gave me the desire to participate in social activities – which looking back, bordered on the irresponsible. Patrick Octave and Gladstone (my best man) were great friends of mine and they were both party animals. It was inevitable therefore, that I became a part of the roaming band of brothers at weekends. However, we were always mindful of where we went. Trying as best we could to visit places that were trouble free but somehow it was not always possible. Discretion did not always equal success. It was clear that our indulgence was an infringement that the British public was not about to accept. There was therefore every indication that our habits would not be tolerated. It was obvious that our traditions were in danger of getting us into serious trouble.

After years of hassle, I decided in the end to heed the pleas of my wife, whose concern for my safety was paramount; especially since there were occasions when colleagues were charged with drug offences that they were not guilty of. It was not unusual to find people in courts for possession when they were totally innocent. I realised that I was blessed with the good fortune of having a wife whose patience, tolerance and love paved the way in giving us the solid base our marriage has today.

It must be stressed that apart from work, we were undergoing a period of change that eventually would determine how we settled in our new society. Our habits and mannerisms clearly were incompatible with the British way. They were quick to remark how different we were. Naturally, and without a doubt, that is very true. We are different and what is more we like the way we are.

The British never change their ways when abroad. They bring with them a tradition all their own, yet we were expected to be treated like little children that must be seen but not heard.

We are an outgoing, vibrant, exuberant people, a product of the tropical climes from whence we came. To be seen only as wages slaves is depressingly absurd. Poor we may be but we are a proud people and demand to be treated with respect. The great problem arose from the fact that whatever we did was seen as below par and to be discouraged. That was really the bone of contention. We answered the call to live and work here and without a shadow of a doubt we did, not to give away traditions of our own. These traditions were primary to a healthy social existence for us. To be denied the right to express ourselves with confidence and to our satisfaction was in my mind a travesty of justice. We, as a visible minority, lived in a society with severe drawbacks and disadvantages namely substandard housing, limited opportunities and jobs no one wanted, such as the railways, the buses, hospitals, factories and the underground, our task was far from easy. We experienced conditions which can only be regarded as wretched.

All the more reason why we needed our weekends – if only to keep body and soul together, to render a sense of joy to what was then a dismal existence.

Today we look back with a degree of smugness at the sea change of this vibrant 'musical' city and feel that we, the minority, have contributed largely to what it is now. Without doubt our infectious habit has caught on, big time.

THE DIFFICULTY OF
BEING A FOREMAN

In the initial months of becoming a foreman, I realised that I had bitten off far more than I could possibly chew. The sheer horror of working with people who were very unhappy to have us in their midst- where coping with staff problems at every level. Those you give orders to and those you receive orders from – seemed very much like climbing Mount Everest and which was a hard lesson to be learnt.

I was partly aware of the new undertaking, its negative elements and what the end result might be. Taking promotion in as short a time as I did and without any knowledge of railway work (outside of the training period of three weeks which we were allotted) would naturally set me at a distinct disadvantage and there would be difficulties. What I was oblivious of and simply did not bargain for, was the venom and resentment that came with this new venture.

Originally I set my sights only on the financial benefits which I would derive from my promotion, rather than how best I was able to cope with other aspects of the job, such as man management. It was, looking back, the wrong set of priorities. I was never in a position of authority before and was alarmed at the huge difference of attitude changing one uniform for another would make.

As a station man, life was comparatively easy. No one took a second look or paid any particular attention to you. The task of washing tiles or sweeping platforms did not warrant any special consideration. Making the elevation as I did was a totally different matter. Suddenly I was viewed with suspicion; I was now part of management and therefore cannot be trusted. By far the most unacceptable feature of all though, was the knowledge that us three Caribbean lads were doing a job which many regarded as one for senior players and should never been given to comparative green horns like us. That created a massive amount of resentment that lasted for about four years. Travelling around as I did on the

Northern Line in my new capacity, I did not only find the situation uncomfortable but at times wretched. We were three *'coloured boys'* in a job which we were incapable of doing. The reception I got from staff was both frosty and indifferent. Much of the flack we sustained came mainly from inspectors and station masters who objected to *'those people'* coming here and being handed jobs they were not fit to do. The other area, which I found problematic, was dealing with staff at a lower level. As if that was not enough, we had the serious task of coping with the general public.

I must be totally honest in saying that much of the criticism levelled at us at that time carried some merit. It cannot be denied that much of what was said about us happened to be true. Many of my Caribbean colleagues were without the benefit of railway knowledge. Before I became a foreman it never occurred to me that I would take an interest in the workings of trains. Set against that, were those inspectors and station masters who have spent many years plying their skills at something they cared about deeply. Coming in as we did with none or hardly any railway skills could hardly have appealed to their best nature. For many of them, this was an intrusion and they were only too pleased to let their feelings be known. The attitudes shown to us ranged from total silence to open abuse. I would go to large stations and in many cases I would be ignored totally. To a great extent I was invisible. The communication lines between the operating staff and me in many instances was non-existent. Smaller stations were far and away better places to be. At least you were in charge. However, it was not always sweetness and light. Giving instructions to staff, especially those that resented your presence, made the task of supervision very difficult. *"What is this job coming to?"* was an everyday parlance.

We were new and some people treated us as though we were from another planet. Folks would shout at you when speaking, not because they were angry, it was as if they thought it was the only way we could understand them; or they would lean in your direction, with their hand to their ear, a very stereotypical reaction. *"Why did you come here?"* was a frequent but tiresome question. However, the one I found most amusing was, *"I cannot tell you people apart. You all look alike!"*

In the grand scheme of things, there were folks who showed kindness and warmth which made the difference and there were those who were always willing to help – *'come what may'*. However, the ones who could not or would not accept us in any form or shape were more than happy in going to any length to maximise our discomfort. I have had station masters whose rejection of my presence was nothing less than brutal. Others showed breathtaking arrogance. I was told at Edgware once by a station master, *"What the hell is he here for? I don't want him here. What use can he be to me other than making tea?"* I informed him that I was not a drinker of tea (I lied) and was not prepared to make any for anyone. He declared. *"In that case he has no bloody use whatever"*.

Needless to say, I denied myself for the entire time I was there from having a cuppa but it was a triumph for me. One thing was certain, I was positive I was never going to make that horrible little man, a cup of tea. Incidents were many and there were times when the only alternative was to swallow your pride and carry on. I was governed by the principle – what cannot be cured must be endured – riding backwards was not an option, I was a family man and I knew where my responsibility lay.

Some of the more serious instances of unfair play were having station masters issuing instructions to staff through us that led to acrimony. On one occasion I was told to see that staff carry out duties that they were not scheduled to do; something that created hostility and reflected badly on us. On another occasion I instructed a station woman to carry out a task which she objected to.

"How dare you give me work that I am not supposed to do? You've only been in this country for a short time and already just because you are wearing a silly uniform; you think you own the place".

I calmly informed her that it was orders from the boss. I was only following his instructions. She stormed out and confronted him who embarrassingly told her to forget it but he did not forget to give me a mouthful.

"You are a supervisor – your job is to supervise. I gave you an order and I expect you to carry it out. What the hell do you think you are wearing that uniform for?

"Not to give information to staff that would get me into trouble", I replied. His was a case of knowing he was wrong but still trying to be a bully.

The biggest difficulty that we endured was without doubt – dealing with the general public. Conflict was not an everyday occurrence but incidents were far too many for comfort. I recall asking a passenger at Old Street station to vacate the premises as there were no more trains – "How dare you tell me what to do in my own Country. I don't take orders from niggers". He was adamant he was not leaving, forcing me to take emergency measures to remove him.

Hampstead is another area where the rich and mighty reside and there was always the occasion when someone would let you know that you don't count for much. One of my staff alerted me to a woman passenger who apparently fell on the platform in an attempt to board a tube train. Her injuries were not substantial, however, she was shaken by the fall and wanted to complain to the person in charge. She was most indignant and was definitely not prepared to discuss the matter with me; *"What is this country coming to?"* She turned to the station man. *"Please, please, get me someone with a bit of intellect. I am not prepared to deal with any Tom, Dick or Harry".* She was positive she would have nothing to do with me. That meant I was forced to get the station master to deal with a situation I could easily have dealt with.

Another incident that springs to mind was the booking clerk calling down to me at Burnt Oak station with the information that the fire brigade had arrived at the station, wanting to know if we had a problem. I was not aware of a fire or any incident that would require assistance of such nature. I informed the clerk that no help was needed; accepting the obvious that it may have been a false alarm which was not of our making. Moments later the fire chief came down. We chatted for a while, he was satisfied that the call could have come from another source. While we were in conversation, he observed a smouldering on the track, (something that happens from time to time). He extinguished it, conceded to me it was an error and departed. Later that day, much to my surprise, I received a call from my group station master, informing me of how much trouble I was in. According to the fire people, I called them out and in my haste to extinguish the smouldering; I was prepared to throw a bucket of water on the track. As a matter of knowledge, the first and most fundamental piece of information you receive from your training is the importance of the live rail and how to deal with it. For anyone foolhardy enough to throw a bucket of water on 660 volts of electricity is obviously inviting instant death. Yet my station master seemed very much to believe the fire chief's story. When asked, his response was; "I am only going by information received". Fortunately, the booking clerk was the one they contacted, or who knows? He might have believed that I was guilty of calling out the fire brigade.

There were two incidents of spitting. One that hit the target and the other I was able to avoid mainly because of the first experience; an experience that stays with you for as long as life lasts, if only for its ugliness. I was standing at the ticket barrier one evening at Leicester Square, talking to a collector when I felt a presence behind me, I looked around and there was a woman in close proximity to where I was. I turned to face the person, believing that she wanted information relating to travel. However, instinctively I realised that an impending problem was about to ensue. Her blood shot eyes and her cold, piercing stare told me immediately all I wanted to know but before I could react, I felt her warm, unpleasant spittle smack on the side of my face. I was in a confused state of disarray. It was a combination of shock, annoyance and anxiety. Shocked by the suddenness of it, annoyed by the temerity of this woman's action and anxious at what she might do next. My reaction was to simply keep her at bay and as I pushed her away she slipped and fell.

As good fortune would have it, my station master, a Mr. Sylvester who was in the vicinity, came around the corner just as she regained her footing and without a word of warning, she walloped him sending him down on one knee. We subsequently managed (with some difficulty) to restrain her only to find out from the police that she had no fixed abode and was someone who had a history of depression and ill health. As a result no further action was taken. Nevertheless that did not take away the horror of that particular moment, an experience I would never forget. After the incident I asked my station master if he would have believed me if I had told him that this unsavoury act was without provocation. He smiled and told me with a degree of honesty, that he would have found it difficult to believe my story had he not been smacked himself without a reason.

There was another occasion when someone attempted to do the same. It was without success as I anticipated his intentions. It was a case of 'once bitten, twice shy'. His was an act of cowardice. He was more concerned in escaping than anything else. As a result he posed no serious threat.

There were many moments dealing with problems when my better judgement got me out of serious situations. I learned quickly to adapt an attitude that was comparatively safe and fully reliable. The same was true working with staff and after a while, my presence, which was hardly bearable initially, became acceptable and at some stations, very welcomed.

Working to break down barriers was never an easy task to accomplish; but, once achieved, life became far more comfortable. However there was still so much more to understand about the average English person, especially the peculiarity of their ways; that strange temperament that 'ebbed and flowed'. How can someone engage you in conversation one day only to ignore you totally the next? Being of a placid nature myself, I found it difficult to comprehend. I met one such character at Belsize Park. He hardly had a decent word to say to me all the years I visited that station, yet one day I walked into the mess room and was greeted by him as though we were buddies, insisted we have a drink and exclaimed gustily while we were doing so, that he had nothing against West Indians, it was the other bastards that he did not care for. Such remarks were widespread and vividly illustrated the insincerity and dishonesty that sometimes were part and parcel of everyday existence.

What was important for me was that I tried to do the job as best I could. Railway work was never easy, there was always something new to learn. Working with some members of staff make it seems excessively more difficult. Conversely, let us not forget those that helped us to settle and showed great consideration over those very trying years. Our resolve paid great dividends and suddenly things became easier. We were no longer strangers; we became part of a system which worked successfully in producing excellent members, such as foremen, inspectors, station masters, and even divisional inspectors. I believe our efforts have certainly not been in vain. In the process of learning and understanding the job, I was always mindful of presenting a clear and impeccable image as I possibly could. My main motto was always to be someone who was capable of doing the job of work that I had undertaken as well as I possibly could. To work hard to be honest to people and to show them respect. Suffice it to say that respect was not always reciprocated. However, I held fast to the view that a pleasing nature and a convivial attitude would always receive favourable results and that was very much in evidence in the latter years.

COPING WITH WORK AND FAMILY RESPONSIBILITIES

The job of relief foreman was becoming more and more interesting. To deal with the general public and very often-awkward staff, was never easy. As time went by however, I found my ability to cope with problems improved. Moving from station to station was an important function. The nature of the job was such that you were seldom in one place for more than a fortnight.

My wife was now pregnant with our first child and although the flat was relatively comfortable, it was never big enough for more than two people. It became quite clear to us that sooner or later we would have to strive for larger accommodation. With the birth of my son Colin in August of 1961, we found the added furniture of crib, pram and pushchair simply too much for the already limited space that existed. Something had to be done – and soon.

Supermarkets did not invade us at that time. It was an era of small businesses; shopkeepers knew their customers and vice versa and by and large the personal touch was very effective. We found someone very reliable for our groceries. Every Friday evening she would carefully pack and deliver, without fail. She was French and a nicer person you could not meet anywhere. We developed something of a friendship over the years and when she lost her husband it became a test of her resolve. It was not far from Christmas and when we invited her to spend Christmas Day with us she readily accepted. She left very late that evening singing the highest praises. It was for her, one of the best Christmases she had spent for as long as she could remember. Some months later she also lost her dog. Her grief for that animal was simply amazing. She wept for what seemed like ages. It was unfortunate that she had lost both husband and pet in so short a time and perhaps that compounded her grief but it was sad to see that her grief for the dog was greater than that of her husband.

They were other things to which I had to attend. My wife was now pregnant with our daughter, Karen. She was born in January of 1964. My thoughts by now were totally focused on larger accommodation. Greta who introduced me to the flat in the first place, kept reminding me in hints, that she did not like the idea of kids running about over her head. Since she lived directly under us there was no way of avoiding that particular problem. It was very much time to get out.

My course was now finished. I was the proud owner of a diploma in engineering and actively began seeking ways of a transfer from operations to the workshop. One needed to be a member of the engineering union to have access to such and unless you were employed in that field, your chances of becoming a member were almost zero. It was a closed shop. I was aware of the difficulties therein; as a result, it was not my major option. My concern at that time was primarily to have accommodation more suitable for my growing family. My search took me everywhere.

It was the era of council flats. Everyone wanted one. It was also a period when elections were won or lost based upon the amount of homes or flats the Government was able to build. The rules of getting one were not easy. The qualifying period took many years and it was a case of stand in the queue. That council house culture carried with it many social problems, compounded by the unnecessary restrictions placed on us by landlords 'no Irish, no Blacks no dogs' embargo, that more than anything else prompted Caribbean People to begin buying their own homes. It was strictly a case of necessity. Although it solved our accommodation needs, it created another serious problem. English folks did not enjoy having 'Coloured' neighbours; for fear that it would 'lower the tone' of the area, thus causing the price of their homes to fall. That being so, it created in many areas, a mass exodus of white families not wanting to be living next door to Blacks. As a result it became a necessary option for many Caribbean families to acquire homes of their own.

'White Flight' as it was then called, became an advantage rather than a handicap. Renting, with all its drawbacks and restrictions benefited no one and although taking a mortgage carried a tremendous burden, the end result was favourable in more ways than one. Owning a home was not only an achievement, it carried with it a sense of pride; coupled with the fact that many *'Immigrants'* were by now creating a family or sending for the loved ones they left behind - evidently, a new focus was in prospect. As a young man growing up, my parents always indicated that one of the first objectives of a young person is to get a roof over one's head – it was a theme that was a universal fact throughout the Caribbean, so it was never difficult to see it becoming a priority for many. However, getting a mortgage became the proverbial *'mountain'* to climb. Wages were small and as a result it was almost impossible to acquire the finance in order to purchase. Equally it was impossible to borrow from banks that were simply in no mood to accommodate us. It there fore required a special bond between friends and relatives in order to combat the obstacles that were set in our paths. To raise capital for the venture, a membership ring was formed. It was called *'Partnership'* or *'Box'*, where each member involved paid cash into one confidential source who at suitable intervals returned cash to the members, subject to the members' wishes and in order of priority. By far the most ambitious scheme devised was the silent partnership idea. Two people would act jointly in getting a mortgage, only to have their names rescinded subsequently. That left the legal owner the task of ownership. Much of what was done carried some measure of risk. Trust was the all-important factor, which in some cases was severely betrayed. Ultimately, nevertheless, much was achieved. Communities were formed around the city but most importantly it began to remove the dependency of renting, especially from those outrageous and exploitative landlords whose attitude toward us was simply contemptuous.

My own situation was completely different. I had no money, so buying a home was out of the question. You can understand my consternation and total amazement when in searching for accommodation I discovered somewhere quite suitable but with the familiar 'no Irish, no Blacks, no dogs' tag to it. That address was 77 Lennox Road, Finsbury Park and somehow it had a familiar ring to it. That evening I got in and asked my wife about the address. She confirmed my suspicions. It was none other than our shopkeeper friend, Mrs Hussey. My confidence in human nature took a severe bashing that day. How can a decent and seemingly honest person such as she, be indulging in racist behaviour? She had, over the years, satisfied us that she was a fair and caring person, until now. When confronted, she did nothing more than hang her head in shame. That was the end of a good friendship. It is still my view – even now, that she was no more than a good person following an unsavoury trend that existed at the time; one that would always be damaging to the human cause as long as it lasts.

I had just started my duty at Warren Street one afternoon when a Jewish colleague rushed into the office, overwhelmed with delight. He had just won fifty pounds on the horses. His enthusiasm was electric. He boasted of his success and informed me that it was tantamount to printing money. Because of my great need to accrue cash, I was easily persuaded to become a punter. Since I knew absolutely nothing about horses and did not take any interest in studying 'form', my selections certainly did not impress many around me. Beginners luck played an important part however and within six months of punting, one Saturday afternoon I won the princely sum of 300 pounds for a five shillings each-way accumulator. I was in ecstasy and although some of my friends poured scorn on my selections, success was achieved. I was then able, for the first time, to open a bank account.

My kids were now growing up and the flat that I still occupied had become inadequate. Realising the situation, I was determined to purchase a home. The possibility of ever getting a council flat was very remote which left me with very little alternative. I managed to raise a level of cash, which I felt would give me a start. I understood the enormity of the task ahead but for the sake of my family I was certain there was no other alternative.

PURCHASING A HOME;
LOSS OF A FRIEND

On my voyage to England on the 'SS Venezuela', a large and powerful liner with a capacity of many hundreds of passengers, one man stood out like a beacon. He was self assured, confident, funny and possessed a tremendous personality. Such a person was Gladstone Austin. The journey was long and arduous to many of us but to him, the entire trip appeared to be one massive joy ride. I met Gladstone on the second day of my travel and long before that evening was over, I knew that a long and successful friendship was imminent.

Gladstone was a dapper dresser with much enthusiasm and energy and unlike many of us; he was never ill at ease. He consciously or otherwise used those qualities to win over those he made contact with. Elan my friend, was never one for over exuberance and getting to know someone who seemed to have the ability to enjoy every moment of his life, was as refreshing as it was useful. It offered me an opportunity to see the journey in a more relaxed manner and helped me considerably to quell my own anxieties. Meeting someone so self-assured not only boosted my own confidence but made the entire trip far more desirable. Our friendship gathered momentum to the extent that it was obvious even before we arrived in England, that nothing would stop our relationship from prospering.

Our discussions about the future were many and varied and once in London our relationship bonded and we developed a strong sense of brotherhood. He became my barber, my confidant and a trustworthy companion. Our compatibility grew as the months went by and so he became my fun seeking, party going, partner in crime and when I decided to take Gloria's hand in marriage, it was a foregone conclusion that he would be the fittest person – even among my senior friends – to be my best man.

Like me, he was very focused in getting out of rented accommodation. We both knew that it was very unlikely that we would ever be able to acquire a council flat and as a result we began to compete in raising the necessary finance in order to make that purchase a reality.

That was a race I could never win since I was now a married man with two kids and he was still a bachelor. However, since he was such a wonderful friend, it was a contest I did not mind losing and when he informed me of his purchase, I could not help being overjoyed – after all, it was an achievement and as friends go, I was happy to know that his venture had succeeded.

Simultaneously however, I began to notice signs of difficulties ahead. Since I was oblivious of any problems or reasons for his behaviour, I became baffled and began to wonder. What emerged out of all this was simply amazing. His visits began to dwindle, his reluctance to communicate became quite conspicuous and for the first time it occurred to me that our friendship was in doubt. In one of our now very rare discussions he informed me that his newly acquired property was "strictly private". I took that to mean that he was not prepared to rent to anyone. Since it was never an intention of mine to seek any kind of assistance from him, I found his remarks totally strange. He above everyone else knew what my plans were. I was in the process of finding a place of my own. My plans were never in doubt. Although I was not quite ready, I certainly was not prepared to move from one rented accommodation to another.

In the light of what was taking place, I decided to take the initiative to monitor our friendship, to see where it was going and sure enough my perception proved correct. My good and gracious pal had decided to bring our friendship to a sudden and abrupt conclusion. Six marvellous years of the most excellent relationship began to unravel simply because of one small degree of success on his part. It seemed incomprehensible that friendship so meaningful and of the calibre and stature that ours was, could be rescinded for such small gains. Yet since there was no quarrel, no rancour or disagreement of any kind that I was aware of - what could have brought on such a reaction? Was it merely an act of selfishness? Or was it simply a case of friendship running out of steam? Whatever it was, it would be difficult for me to say since I was not privy to my friend's rationale. What was of greater concern to me was the fact that I was unable to judge correctly the true character and nature of this person that I gave trust to.

The vital components of friendship as I understand it are integrity, loyalty and honesty. These are important attributes to any good relationship. To have these qualities trampled upon in an insensitive, inconsiderate and callous manner was woefully sad indeed.

Life and maturity has taught me many things. One of those is that friendship is different things to different people. In the case of my former friend, Gladstone, maybe his was one of convenience. In that context, I was glad it ended as it did. Those who know me well – and there are a few – understand implicitly what I stand for. I believe in honesty and respect. It is what I try to give to people. In the case of my ex-friend, the respect that I gave to him was not reciprocated.

ACQUIRING MY HOME

The public bath culture, which was very much in evidence in my early years, seemed extraordinary to many people, but especially to those of us from the Caribbean. Coming as we did from the tropics we were never able to understand the idea of weekend baths. Yet that was the custom of the inhabitants of this land, who turned up in great numbers, especially on a Saturday morning for this unusual ritual.

Rooted in that culture perhaps, was the reason why so many houses were built without the important facility of a bathroom. The heat of the sun and the very nature of our environment demanded that washing regularly was a normal practice of ours, a habit that got unfavourable comments from our white counterparts, who viewed our constant washing as both unhealthy and unnecessary.

My circumstances - living above Greta - were becoming intolerable. With my family increasing - two children at this stage - I was constantly reminded by her of the need to acquire somewhere more suitable for my family. Greta or not, I knew it was time to move on and the only way to go, was to strive for a home of my own. Although our savings were not substantial, it was adequate enough to take that quantum leap of finding a place of our own.

Our search began in earnest and our primary objective was to find somewhere with all the amenities intact. That obviously meant finding a house with a bathroom. The task of house hunting was far from easy, but our perseverance and determination paid off in the end. Thus at long last we found a house in Palmers Green that satisfied our needs. Although there was no overt jubilation we were nevertheless quietly contented that this venture was a major achievement in our lives. Naturally we found the task of repaying the mortgage somewhat horrendous, but it was a challenge that we had to face, and with the help of my mother in law - who paid us a rent, we were able to combat our financial problems satisfactorily. Above all we were now proud owners of our own home.

It was without doubt a new beginning. The physical energy, the enormity of the task, the endless obstacles to overcome, the bickering I endured from Greta and all the related problems were now laid to rest. Perhaps easily the greatest struggle that I may have encountered (many other would have had similar experiences) throughout my existence in this country, was advancing from renting to home ownership. The obstacles and frustrations that were manifest in this endeavour were very real indeed. The ability to acquire funds for such a task. Finding suitable accommodation and having it approved by all the concerned parties was simply an enormous undertaking. However, once achieved, it brought a significant sense of satisfaction that is unbeatable. For the first time I was able to feel like a responsible parent who was able to give to my family the freedom and space so necessary for their natural development.

Purchasing a home was a monumental attainment for anyone who was fortunate enough to do so. The difficulties were it was not seen as a popular undertaking in an era when the indigenous population depended largely on obtaining a council flat. That immigrants were able in so short a time to accomplish the serious task of home purchasing brought fierce and prolonged resentment from various parts of the community. Nevertheless the advantages for so doing far outweighed the obstacles that were apparent and although I was now confronted with the burdensome matter of a mortgage (which many found prohibitive) nothing was able to dim or destroy the pride and deep satisfaction I felt for a job well and truly done.

Shortly after our purchase we received news from Guyana that was far from good. My mother was ill, that was not what I wanted to hear, especially at a time when I was completely cash strapped. I kept in constant touch with the situation and hoped and prayed that she would survive long enough for us to be reunited again. We suggested a holiday but she would have none of it. My sister alerted me to the impending problem, yet when I got word of her demise it was indeed a severe shock to my system. I experienced a deep sense of loss and a kind of uselessness prevailed around me. I was miles away, unable in any meaningful way to assist. That, with the other problems of a newly purchased home, tested my mental stability to the fullest.

Perhaps the single reason that compounded my grief above all else was the promise that I made to her - that we would have been reunited within five years - would now remain unfulfilled. Looking back, it is easy to see how rapidly priorities changed in this new environment of which I was now a part, particularly considering the circumstances of that era. My preoccupation and priority was simple – finding the best way to provide comforts that were suitable for my young family and me. As a result, my focus and all my energies – not to mention my limited finance – were channelled towards this goal. It was almost eight years since I had departed my homeland and the reality that things would never be the same – that I would never see my beloved Mother ever again – was now taking hold. Two options were now open to me: either immerse myself in a state of remorse or consider my blessings and to recall how fortunate I was to have had such a wonderful mother like her.

My mother's death taught me to be strong against all adversities and above all to conquer them. There is still a sense of guilt somewhere in my subconscious thoughts, that I should have made provision for such an eventuality, but my mother was always of a forgiving nature, a kind considerate and loving person; someone who would always understand. I owe a huge debt of gratitude to her. Never ever would I be able to forget her unselfish contribution in time of need. Her generosity cannot be faulted. She gave freely, and when she did it was always with the greatest of pleasure. Thank you dear mother! I still think lovingly of you. May you rest in eternal peace.

A STARTLING REVELATION
TO A MATURE ADULT

One Sunday evening, some months later, I was on duty at Colindale station when I had a most mind-blowing experience; one that changed my mental concept in a very comprehensive way. Politically, I was not totally naïve but I had no sense of history. By that I meant African History. I knew nothing about the slave trade and the ramifications of it. It never occurred to me until then, that at least I should have known something about my *'Africaness'* – the history of my ancestors and the merits of knowing of my African past. I was in for a major shock. There was hardly anyone around, Colindale being a quiet place, especially on a Sunday, when I heard footsteps and this charming and most friendly man appeared. He smiled readily and asked mostly unimportant questions. He apparently was an inspector of police in Portugal – bored and with nothing to do he had wandered off from Hendon Police Training College and found himself at the station. We chatted about a variety of things and to be truthful I felt reasonably comfortable in his company.

I told him I was in the process of coming to terms with the death of my mother. Explaining how I was unable to attend her funeral and how awful I felt about it. It was then I saw the other side of the man. Still smiling, he said: "Of course if you people were clever enough and were able to run your country efficiently, you would not have to be here. Would you?" "To tell you the truth" he continued, "Black People are just stupid, brainless beings".

My immediate reaction was one of dismay. He was still smiling and in a way I tried matching him with a smile of my own. I must admit at that instant I was totally void of any constructive retort. "Are you implying that we are all stupid people?" I asked.

"Of course", he carried on, "Let's face it young man – what have you lot contributed to civilisation? Absolutely nothing; the only thing noteworthy about Africans, is that they make very good slaves".

I was hurt. Here was a man without cause or reason, who was quite willing to insult not only me but also the entire African race, seemingly just for the fun of it. Perhaps what was most frustrating was my inability to respond in any meaningful way.

"You are very wrong about the African race," I said. Still smiling, he responded.

"You people are at the bottom of the pile because that is your natural place – you need brains to be at the top and that's what Africans don't have - in any case, someone has to be at the top and someone has to be at the bottom and that unfortunately is your place".

He never waited for a reply and moved very quickly away, leaving in his wake a dispirited and humiliated member of the human race – it became imperative for me as an option to know more about myself – more about the history of Africa. It was not difficult to understand that right up to then, I was a product of what I would call a 'Tarzan mentality'; gullible and childlike. Yet I suspected very early in my childhood that there was something wrong with my thinking process. I saw the World and all its activities through the eyes of Europeans. Deep down I felt that there was something artificial or veneer about such a concept.

As a young man, I enjoyed reading and it was taken for granted that any literature of any substance or quality was written by Europeans. I must admit that I was very impressed with the image of Tarzan, "King of the Jungle". He was a most incredible man. Growing up in the jungle did not stop him from knowing all the answers. He talked to the animals – sometimes he had to show them who was the boss. He solved all of Black Africa's problems and made all the animals, from the biggest to the smallest, aware of his presence, especially when he yelled. He must have had pretty sore hands, swinging on those vines all over the continent, always with the greatest of success – since we were considered Apes; it was not difficult to work out who he was king of. One thing was manifestly clear; he had the vision, the mental and physical prowess to be superior to all those Africans around him. Every now and again I would ask myself why Tarzan was not an African. After all, the environment was more akin to those who originated from the area but that would not have been good for the myth that Tarzan was meant to portray. That, by and large, was the measure of my consciousness. I grew up being told by the priest that it was a mortal sin to be absent from Mass on a Sunday and we believed him. He forbade us to see certain films; afraid of what it might do to our minds and he was always ready in a controlling way to keep us as meek and subservient as possible.

We were told if we were to be good Christians, we must follow the rules. We must be obedient, work diligently, respect our masters, and perhaps if we were really good, we would reap our rewards in heaven. Somehow, I accepted these conditions with the greatest of reservations, but accepted I did, since no one presented an alternative view. The question I asked myself, was why in a world of plenty, such abundance of wealth and riches, I would have to wait for my share of 'milk and honey' in another place. Since no one was able to give tangible evidence of that promise – after all no one ever came back to tell us – how best was I able to believe it? Was it merely the proverbial 'pie in the sky'?

The truth is, Caribbean people, as a whole, take their religion very seriously. My parents and most of the villages were true believers. Spiritualism is fundamentally a part of our physiological make up. Our Sundays, the period of lent and especially Good Fridays were days of solemnity, fasting and prayer. How different it was when I arrived here. The significance of those occasions seemed to have been lost completely. Churches were half-empty and Good Friday was seen as just another day. Can you imagine how I felt when I was rostered to work on Good Friday here?

It would appear to me on face value anyway that the milk and honey theory hardly seemed to apply to the indigenous people of England, which obviously meant that religion was different things to different people.

As kids, the great attraction for us was to be allowed to go to see cartoons at our local cinema (matinee). Naturally, we needed to be on our best behaviour in order to be allowed the opportunity. Donald Duck, Mickey Mouse and the rest, represented good entertainment for us. What was always on display was the imagery of a fat black woman, with her head tied and with bulging eyes, being made fun of; thus reinforcing the manifestly clear notion of our uselessness as we watched those 'darkies' as they were called, again with their bulging eyes and always appearing to be in a state of fear while their white contemporaries were always in command.

Absolutely nothing was said to suggest otherwise but what was significantly clear was the superiority factor in every aspect. Without any doubt we were the underdogs economically, socially inferior and politically inept. What was obviously intended was to create a psychological impact on our young minds and what is more it was a grand success.

The emergence of Joe Louis, the heavyweight champion of the world, was the one single reason for hope in a world that denied us so much. He was a hero, an icon and someone who was much revered, and although he was somewhat naive, he raised expectations and brought much joy and happiness to his people by performing in the ring with ruthless efficiency, thus assaulting that psychological impact on our minds.

We were taught about the Greek Civilisation at school; English history and literature were the norm – Shakespeare, Dickens, Hawkins, Drake and Nelson come readily to mind. Nothing about the African past was ever mentioned and I would wager a bet that most of our teachers knew nothing about Africa other than to describe it as the 'Dark Continent'. We were depicted very often as savages. We wore our 'Negro' tag with great dignity and so when the 'Mother Country' beckoned, most of us felt comfortable with the idea of coming home. England was home for many of us – but many of my colleagues to this day are in a state of confusion and cannot or will not accept their African heritage. Some are blissfully unaware of who they are and are happy to remain so, there are others with knowledge that would be useful to raising awareness necessary to advance our cause but are complacent and reluctant to do so. We the African people, both in the Diaspora and on the Continent have been denied information of our past for far too long. We are the only race with such a disadvantage. To say that it is wrong would be a colossal understatement. Knowledge of the past sustains the present, so we can go into the future with our confidence intact and self-esteem lifted. Indirectly, I thank my Portuguese adversary for triggering my self-consciousness. At least now I know a little bit of who I really am.

Today we know that African History was plagiarised and used by some other races as its own. We know that Africans were the first contributors of excellence in the field of medicine, architecture, astrology, religion and more. We know that no attempt has been made to establish and give credit to geniuses such as Imhotep, Amen and others – and that the African's history was the only one to be totally and deliberately suppressed.

FIRST RETURN VISIT TO GUYANA

I was now preparing to return to my homeland for the first time in eleven years. I was overcome with excitement. Who would have thought it would take me that long to return; the years simply melted away. However, quite unlike the way I arrived in England by boat, I was now returning in style by plane. Those eleven short years taught me a great deal about life and how not to take anything for granted. As I sat on the plane, heading towards the Caribbean sun and reflecting on things past and present, I was very conscience of many broken promises, shattered dreams and unfilled pledges that were made and wondered if the gods of good fortune had dealt me an unfavourable hand. It was then that I fully realised that growing up had a responsibility of its own. I had taken on a mantle of adulthood. No more was I the fun-seeking creature of pastimes. I had the good fortune of a healthy family, a newly acquired home and more over, I was now settling fairly adequately in my new environment, London. It was clearly time to start appreciating my blessings and working towards using my resources and energies to advance my own cause and not to look back.

This was the first opportunity to talk to my mother, in spirit that is and to see relatives and old friends. Generally speaking, the visit was one of mixed emotions. Almost all the people I knew intimately had by now left the country; and the way I envisaged things there had changed dramatically. The landscape in my memory that sustained me over the years no longer existed. No more were the places I played as a boy. Dreams were shattered as a result – nevertheless I was more than impressed with what I saw on that visit. There was something about the place that was most encouraging. Guyana had assumed a vibrancy that I had not seen before. Homes were built where once swamplands were, new roads were built and new ones proposed.

The University was most resplendent in its new grounds and generally there was a prevailing sense of expectation about the Country. So upbeat was the place that the 'feel good' factor was very much in place. I also got the chance to visit my mother's grave. I explained to her how sorry I was to be absent when she needed me and more than anything else, I felt wretched for breaking the promise I made to see her again, which turned out to be a terrible miscalculation. For some inexplicable reason so many of us felt that going abroad, achieving great things and returning home within five to ten years was possible. Little did we know that for most of us it became a lifetime struggle and for some only survival. In a way I felt a sense of relief being there. I was full of her presence, as if her spirit reigned over me. My thoughts for her are ever abiding and I know she still keeps watch over me.

I returned to England from Guyana in jubilant mood. Full of enthusiasm for the progress that was being made and felt sure that with the right policies – it was only a matter of time before Guyana becomes a major force in the region.

Back in London we were concerned about another problem. My wife was not enjoying the best of health; something that worried us to a large extent and as a result we did not pay adequate attention to Colin's (our son) general progress in school. We as parents were very active in our attendances and showed great interest not only in school activities but also in our child's general development. Growing up, Colin was very small and somewhat reserved – traits that were more of a disadvantage than an asset. He was not one for speaking up or making waves, confiding only in his mother. My personal view of him was that his academic ability was better than average but his school reports - although good, never bore that out. We began to notice his general mood and lack of enthusiasm around the house and pressed by his mum we found out that the natural elevation (up-streaming) he expected did not happen. Urgent investigations from the school revealed a most unsatisfactory response. His automatic up-streaming did not occur because he did not perform well in the key subjects. Our objection to that was fairly obvious. How can a child assessed in the top five of the class be left behind – when others far less talented moved ahead of him? Contesting the unfairness of that decision created problems of its own. It placed a considerable amount of pressure on my son who was forced to remain static for an entire year, and because of our interest we were considered troublesome parents. Our subsequent attempts to move him to another school similarly failed. It was not for want of effort on our part. All roads were blocked in that direction even though we were given every assurance by the head of another schooling that he would be admitted, it never happened. He eventually left school without achieving the required standard necessary for academic excellence and which would propel him automatically into a decent or worthwhile occupation.

Happily with persuasion on our part and with Colin's self-belief in his own ability, he pursued efforts through night school and other education forums to achieve the necessary status for success. That self-sacrifice, determination and hard work paid off in the end. Fortunately he had parents who were keen to see their children achieve. What about those who did not pay such attention? Many of us, who were from the Caribbean, developed an understanding that sending your children to school - that once there; teachers would take care of their every need. The culture was derived from our own experiences. Teachers looked after our welfare and in many ways we were in safe keeping once at school. Perhaps out of that experience parents were less attentive and in my opinion the very reason the period of education sub normal era prevailed in the society as long as it did.

The E.S.N sin bin era was probably the most damaging and ill-conceived system ever devised by the education authorities. Since it is difficult to understand the logic of it, it must be assumed that its purpose was deliberate and it was designed to destroy rather than to create. The children who suffered under this awful system were visible minorities but more so African-Caribbean. Perfectly normal children were subjected to this unfortunate experience, devised by supposedly serious people and educators who should have known better and resulted in large numbers of good talented children falling victim to this absurd plan. If ever there was a vexed question throughout my time in the United Kingdom, it was certainly the E.S.N system. Many voices were raised against it, numerous people forecasted the horror it would bring, yet it was allowed to continue. In the end, large sections of Black children were denied basic education. Many were bitter and frustrated at a system that was never meant to educate and train kids; but to ultimately fail them. Children growing up in a community without any prospects, without hope. How can these children, through no fault of their own, be expected to be good citizens – to show goodwill or be ambassadors, it is very difficult to imagine. What was most incredible was the concept that teachers (who were mainly white) believed that the colour of a child's skin determined their ability to achieve academically. And so large numbers of black kids who may have escaped E.S.N had so little attention paid to them, only to be told some years down the line that they were under achievers. Alarm bells were ringing in opposition to this system. One of the few black teachers, Bernard Coard who wrote a book called ' How the West Indian child is made educational subnormal in the British school system', advanced a serious warning of the repercussions of that policy. He indicated that it would make 'helots' of our kids and begged for change that was ignored. The adage, 'what goes round comes round' – is quite evident today. The errors of yesterday (bad planning) are bound to impact on society today. A generation of children ill-equipped to face the future – without training or qualifications and without hope cannot make decent law abiding citizens. Sadly, these children are now fully-grown adults and are producing children of their own. If society is mindful of its people – all its people, lets us hope this generation of children would not be marginalized as were their parents and that a measure of fairness would prevail, giving all citizens – Black and White – a fair crack of the whip. My own view and of course many others who are on this side of the ethnic barrier, has perceived this policy as vehemently racist. Try as I may, I cannot see it any other way. It was a sordid attempt to create an underclass.

THE QUESTION OF RESPECT

The question of respect has been a major factor throughout my entire life in Great Britain. According to the dictionary, it means to regard; to relate to; to honour; to have consideration for. Those qualities have not been genuinely obvious towards the ethnic minority and especially the African population in this Country. Historically, the inhabitants or British People have never perceived us as normal or ordinary human beings. The manufactured doctrine of racism has prevailed for well over a century and in its wake has become a part of European culture – as natural as fish and chips. White supremacy and control was largely responsible for this calamitous doctrine. For nearly four hundred years misinformation and myth has compounded this philosophy during and after slavery, to the extent that all other races have come to regard us Africans with less respect than we deserve. Scholars of great repute, renowned writers fell over themselves to degrade and debase the African race. Savages, we were called, incapable of any mental or intellectual capacity. It was constantly expressed that the African race did not in anyway contribute to civilisation and by and large we were as a race – inferior. The Christian Church played a pivotal role in advancing this absurd theory as authentic, (one Pope describing us as soulless individuals) and as a consequence, racism became a natural form of existence and was universally accepted.

The sad truth is – Europeans see us as lesser beings, so treating us with indifference is quite normal. I vividly recall a couple of incidents, one where the son of one of my friends went job seeking with his white contemporary. Paul was more scholarly than his white friend but was awarded a less suitable job. Seeing the situation, the lad reported the matter to his white father who told him without remorse that it was correct, that Paul was not *'one of us'* - he was black. The other incident was when I walked in unexpectedly on a work colleague and overheard a conversation of his to a very receptive audience. The theme was *'Black Power'*. African Americans were taking a stand on the way the society to which they belonged treated them. News about *'Black Power'* was everywhere and most of it uncomplimentary. Fred was expounding his theory of what it all meant.

"Blacks were vicious people with nothing but hate in their hearts. Their motives were sinister. It was based primarily on the annihilation of the White race and nothing would get in the way of that". As I entered the mess room, someone alerted him of my presence. He was totally embarrassed. The following day he was all apologetic and insisted that he meant no ill will by his remarks and assured me that there was no racial intent. I informed him that he was entitled to his opinion but I felt in this instance he was wrong. I reminded him of the plight of the African American. Having been emancipated for over a hundred years, basic entitlements were still denied them; lack of jobs, lack of opportunities, voting rights and lots more. That they earned the right to greater autonomy, in a society that they have given blood and tears to help build, and that they were only expressing the shortcomings of a Country which prided itself on being free and fair. Fred showed genuine lack of knowledge of the facts and thought it was worthy of me to enlighten him on the situation.

It was a good feeling to hear him say so. My belief was simple, if I could convince even one European in changing their outlook about us it would be something of an accomplishment.

Three weeks later to my astonishment, there was Fred again. This time to the clerks in the booking office; and what was his theme? *"Those no good black bastards in America whose sole intention was to annihilate all White People..."* The lesson learnt is that some people listen but cannot hear.

Africans from the Caribbean area saw themselves as relics of slavery. Our fore parents were slaves and since we were denied our history, many of us felt and accepted that Europeans were superior in every way. To accept Britain as the mother Country did not require much convincing; for many of us it was an accepted fact. It was no secret that to study and return home was a noble and outstanding achievement. Those returnees demonstrated pride and satisfaction worthy of the Europeans themselves. Their actions and behaviour typified that. Lesser mortals like me looked up to them with a certain degree of awe.

It was only natural, our names and our culture attested to the fact that we were British and proud of it. When we were called to arms, we responded and after the war when we were called to rebuild our Mother Country, it was sweet music to our ears. It became a case of who wanted to remain behind. The reality of coming to live and work in England was very different to our natural expectations. The novelty of seeing so many Caribbean people in London soon subsided and thereafter, the full impact of being a stranger in this new place was evident. To be called a dirty black bastard mainly on the colour of your skin is preposterous. My own experience tells me that Caribbean people's personal hygiene is second to none. To be a natural candidate of suspicion, merely because of your skin colour, for drugs, muggings and theft is wrong as ever it was. We represent at the very least half a million people from the Caribbean yet much of what we do that is positive is hardly ever newsworthy. An English person on holiday in the Caribbean or elsewhere becomes news if an accident occurs, a Prime Minister or other dignitaries from our shores are seldom mentioned when they visit. A cat stuck in a tree gets greater publicity than an election result from our countries. We have the highest percentage of people in prison in proportion to our numbers. The highest percentage unemployed, an unusual proportion in mental hospitals, the most likely people to be harassed, both at work and by the police. All these are unmistakable facts. To be denied jobs or opportunities in business or sport, based entirely on the colour of one's skin is simply unacceptable, yet by and large, that is what the visible minority is subjected to – society's prejudices. Black folks experience two layers of stress; the normal ones of everyday life and the added ones of being visible. Heavy manners indeed! It would be foolish of me to conclude that any society is without its prejudices but what we are faced with is the colour of our skin and it is our skin colour which dictates people's action towards us, an action which is fundamentally more dangerous. This action is based on race and all its negative elements. We do not live in an ideal world but we are in this society and very much a part of it. We the older ones may go back – at least some will but our children and grand children are here to stay. Good governance, unions and institutions of influence that are at the cutting edge of society can make the difference. Rhetoric without substance is meaningless. Example that is worthwhile coupled by sound planning, are some of the requirements for change. We are and will continue to be an asset to any society given the opportunity to do so. We are and always will be, that kind of people.

MOVING ON

The first twelve years of living in London and working with London Transport has shaped my life in a way that I was now able to face the future with greater assurance. The naïve innocent lad from Guyana was replaced by a more mature and conscious individual. I was now beginning to get restless, especially since I failed to get the desired transfer I craved to the engineering section. I needed a change and quickly. My aspiration to travel to the United States for further training was still very much my aim. In order to do so, my financial requirements would have to be vastly improved. News that the Post Office might be the answer to my problems was filtering through. Some of my friends who made the transition were never short in their encouragement for me to move on. Payslips were shown to me, mostly superior to what I was getting and that was incentive enough for me to take the plunge. To say I was sentimental about London Transport was putting it mildly. It was my first and only job since I arrived. My experiences were many. Some good, some less than desirable, especially the years I spent as a foreman. But generally the contacts that I made, the people that I befriended, and more so those that helped me when times were tough can never be forgotten. On leaving the employ of London Transport after twelve years, I was both surprised and delighted by numerous goodwill messages and gifts that I received testimony to the fact that much was accomplished over those years. I shall always be grateful. I give my profound thanks to all of them.

It is said that circumstances alter cases. That saying was never truer than now. I was the proud father of my third child, Claire. With a mortgage to take care of and other pressing financial commitments, the constraints far outweighed any sentimentality that I may have possessed and set against my cash flow problem, I found it financially expedient to move as expressly as possible. Time (old age) was becoming a major factor.

I entered the job as a postman in 1971 and found it totally different from the one I had just left. As a relief foreman I had the freedom of movement, going from station to station, meeting different people and always experiencing changing circumstances. Not so the Post Office. Since Mount Pleasant was considered the biggest sorting office in the world, it was certainly not short in capacity but the general profile of the job meant you were confined. A situation I was never comfortable with and found it less enjoyable. However, since my plans were short term – my stay at the office was to have been three years maximum – I considered it a sacrifice worth making. My overall strategy was to acquire sufficient funds to meet my domestic needs as well as making enough for my American trip. My friend Christopher Streaker was thinking along the same lines. His aim was an electrical course at the same college, so the idea of us travelling together in a sharing capacity was agreed in order to minimise our expenses. It was an achievable task in my estimation, one that I was prepared to make in order to acquire success. Those three years were memorable for one reason only; my total dedication in pursuit of my goal. Long hours at work (overtime), inadequate rest and more work characterised that period. There were three very long years and although a measure of success was achieved by way of savings, there were hardly years that I recall with any degree of pleasure. I made the necessary contact with the college in Long Island and got a favourable response but a series of events were happening around me and what should have been the most productive period of my life, in essence, was perhaps the most torrid.

My plans for America were now on hold. Thanks to the absence of Christopher who was unavailable due to ill health. It became obvious that he could not travel and more so was not able to give an indication of when he would be able to do so. His condition worsened as the months went by and somewhere in my mind I was beginning to feel that the opportunity was slipping away. The deadline for enrolment to the college had long gone. Gone also were the fees that were paid for the commencement of the course. My mother-in-law, who was resident with us and was assisting us financially by way of rent, was far from well. That concerned us greatly, especially my wife and perhaps in some ways her constant worry about her mother's health, contributed to her own ill-health.

Those months slipped by rapidly and with them came the news that my mother-in-law was in a worse way than we first thought. She was found to be terminally ill and on the advice of relatives in Guyana, we sent her home. After her departure the oncoming months were riddled with worry and speculation. My wife, who was not exactly enjoying a rich vein of health at that time, found further deterioration that necessitated surgery. There were a lot of things on my mind but none more than the concerns for my wife. It was without a doubt a case of subordinating my own self-interest for the good of my family but especially my wife. We were hoping against hope that fate would not play the same trick on her as it did on me. That lightning would not strike twice. Alas, it was not to be. Shortly before she was due in hospital, her mother passed away. She was denied the opportunity of seeing her beloved mother again. Those weeks and months were traumatic ones indeed. Shortly after her mother's demise, Gloria was hospitalised. She was full of remorse for not being able to fulfil her role as a senior member of the family. To her it was a heavy loss. That period, without doubt, required a maximum amount of patience, love and understanding. It was the ultimate test of our strength of mind and resilience to enable us to get through that stretch of our domestic life. Thanks to our dedication and our desire to succeed, we were able to do so.

My own objectivity was now in sharp focus. No more was I a young man with thoughts and visions only about myself. My expectations were lowered, my dreams and ambitions diminishing rapidly. My responsibilities took on a new dimension and so did my priorities. I was now a family man with a wife and three children and needed to pay attention to their advancement – to render adequate guidance in order for them to emerge as good solid members of society. That task is far from easy. Good parenting is a combination mostly to do with the gradual development of our offspring. Many of us good, decent, well-meaning parents are often indelicate with the way we handle our kids. Our own strict upbringing is often imposed on them, resulting in serious conflicts. In an environment such as this, greater tolerance is encouraged. Let us not forget the tremendous influence that the environment has on our children. To succeed depends therefore on our ability to adapt to the new way – to be flexible but firm but more importantly, to be there for them when support is needed. Difficult as it is, we as parents are duty bound to try. Very often our task is made all the more horrendous by society's attitude to them. To be told by the schools that a high percentage of them are likely failures. To be seen by the Police as the ones likely to offend. To be told by employers that they are not good enough to hold decent jobs and to almost be twice as good as their European counterparts in sport and other activities is a daunting prospect. Yet these are the pressures that thousands of good 'visible minority' families are subjected to. Such attitudes can only be construed as counter productive. Parents should be rewarded for their energy, patience and good management of their children, yet more often than not they experience despair. Our children must not be taken for granted. Too often that is the case. My own experience tells me so. Twice we have been told not to expect too much from our children. On both occasions they were wrong. The fact that my youngest daughter was told by her teacher that taking 'O' levels was wasting not only her time but also the school's time, is a solid case in point. Not only did she pass but also today she is a graduate and a very successful teacher. Left to the teachers of the school my son attended he would no doubt be doing a less professional occupation but with encouragement and effort and good advice, he is now a successful engineer.

To prejudge children, especially our children, impacts negatively on them and as a result inflicts serious damage to their confidence. We must remember that every member of the human race born has aspirations and ambitions of their own. It is also true that millions will never ever accomplish their aims, largely because circumstances or opportunities may never present themselves but those dreams must never be dulled or impeded by a system that is designed to obstruct progress. That being so it is incumbent on society and especially those who are at the heart of decision making, to create a far more favourable condition than at present exists. We need an even playing field. They are those who are quick to be critical of us. We are supposed to have chips on our shoulders. My response to that is simple; those of us who wear the shoes feel the pinch. The statistics have established without doubt that a higher percentage of our kids leave school prematurely, more than average are in prison or are criminalised, more are unemployed than other races, the same is true for stress and nervous breakdowns. Accident? Hardly! Coincidence? Not likely! These are serious problems that need to be addressed and quickly.

MAINTAINING THE GUYANA LINK

The next twelve years were preoccupied with the mundane task of getting on with life and the business of bringing up our three kids. Money was still in short supply and the temptation for my wife to resume work was very strong indeed. In the end we decided that in the long-term interest of the children it was not prudent to do so. The long hours at work was beginning to take its toll. The children were generally interested in knowing the country of our birth and were asking many questions. Christmas was not far away and I felt jaded and needed to break away, at least for a while from the routine that I set myself. As luck would have it, a friend of mine alerted me to a 'Christmas Special' which was in fact a chartered flight to Barbados and Guyana. The trip was not only good for its affordability; it presented me with an opportunity of taking my daughters to the Caribbean for the first time. My own excitement was sky high. It was a chance to see Guyana again and to re-acquaint myself with relatives and friends alike. It also gave my wife an opportunity to have a spiritual interaction with her mother.

Guyana at that time was very much in turmoil. Forbes Burnham who had been President had just died and Desmond Hoyte now headed the government. The Burnham era at that time was beset by controversy of every dimension. His party was accused of rigging elections, for behaving dictatorial but more crucially for killing Dr Walter Rodney, the popular and charismatic historian and leader of the W.P.A (a party in opposition) and much more. Dr. Rodney, one of Guyana's outstanding sons and a gifted politician who was regarded by many as a legitimate leader in waiting, deepened the gloom and misery that had already existed by his sudden and unfortunate demise. It was a shock to the system. One that I very much doubt Guyana has ever recovered from. Forbes Burnham's general policy to house, feed and clothe the nation in a given time frame was known and well regarded throughout the Caribbean and elsewhere. He was also known as a visionary and a true believer of Caribbean integration. Carifesta was born from that concept and many regarded that as an admirable achievement. However, his philosophy of party paramountcy and his self proclaimed status as a socialist were principally the reasons for Guyana's setback, which ultimately created an atmosphere of suspicion and distrust, both internally and externally. We on this side of the world knew of the problems that existed but nothing or no one prepared me for what I was to experience. Guyana was in political free fall. The gains that I observed on my first visit had all but gone.

Forbes Burnham's policies unfortunately impacted on the country as a whole. His ideology was anathema to Washington whose propensity to be intolerant with upstarts was never in doubt. As a result, retribution was swift. The economy suffered a massive blow from lack of foreign exchange; the results of his internal policies regressed with alarming speed. The banning of certain food items such as flour and split peas considered as a staple diet to the Indian-Guyanese was considered a serious political flaw and only helped to compound an awful situation that was already in place. The end result was a black market scenario which gradually developed and has presided over the country ever since. My own expectations were truly shattered. My disappointment was total. The infrastructure was in disarray and almost everything was in short supply. Worse was the impoverishment of the ordinary people. My friends, who had remained in Guyana, were now all gone.

The environment had changed considerably. Inflation was high and times were generally difficult. Yet the people showed a high degree of resolve and good naturedness throughout our stay, in spite of the difficulties they faced. My kids were seeing an underdeveloped Country for the first time and although they had some reservations, they thoroughly enjoyed the time spent there. It also gave them the opportunity of seeing their cousins and other relatives for the first time. Nevertheless, those weeks were spent explaining away the inadequacies that were so apparent in the country and pointing out why some of the basic things like water and electricity which were taken for granted in England were such a problem in countries such as Guyana. That they were impressed with the physical beauty of the Country was never in doubt, what was uninspiring was the lack of opportunities and progress that the Country was able to make.

POLITICS OF CHANGE

Back in London and thinking of countries such as Guyana, it becomes abundantly clear how different developed countries are as opposed to under developed ones. The economic power and control is so overwhelming that it would take an imagination of huge proportion to fathom where and how a change would ultimately emerge. The machinery that was set all those years ago are still very much in place. Multinationals and conglomerates are forever working in the interest of developed countries. Their agenda is manifestly set to maintain that status quo. Banking, shipping and insurance – have created great benefits for those establishments. So too are our mineral resources which are exploited to a mind-boggling extent. Conversely, Third World Countries under the weight of such awesome might, are forever hoping and forever raising their expectations that foreign investment would ultimately change their lives, that is very often if not always a pipe dream. I grew up in a country, which I am told is unique. It is a country rich in mineral resources and that it was only a matter of time before we would emerge as a prosperous country. I am now in the evening of my years and I still await the miracle. My only hope is that the government of Guyana, in pursuit of political gains, (short term or otherwise) do not allow unscrupulous companies whose only interest is to make a fast buck, creating an environmental catastrophe. There are obvious signs that it is beginning to happen already.

The political landscape in Britain was now experiencing something of a metamorphosis. A new era was born. For the first time the country voted for a woman Prime Minister and with it, a new political spirit. The country and to a large extent the world was engulfed in 'Thatcherism '. The end result was massive change. Companies, establishments of every hue were subjected to one kid of reform or the other. This new mood was all prevailing matched only by the enthusiasm of so many who were given the opportunity for the first time to own their council flats instead of renting. This policy was a complete change from the old tradition, virtually dismantling that culture and swiftly making way for the far more acceptable concept of outright ownership. The political approach being somewhat novel and for many, very refreshing, made changes such as privatisation acceptable. The philosophy for change was so overwhelming; it was obvious that nothing was sacrosanct. The Post Office was no exception. What was once an established institution, with no overt inclination for change and was regarded as a service industry was now moving in the direction of big business. Privatisation was the order of the day and rumours were rife that we were next in line.

Many of the senior staff were worried about the situation especially since many of us were getting to or had passed our 'sell by date' and the news for us was far from pleasing. It soon became apparent that the process of change had begun and new strategies were put in place. New machines and certainly new ideas were everywhere. The perception that we the older ones got was very obvious. We were to become surplus to requirement. Great emphasis was placed on younger heads and it was apparent that the policy of early retirement would soon be established. I personally felt that such a policy was wrong. For an establishment as large as the Post Office to transit from a service industry to a competitive business it would need to evolve with less haste and with a sounder management machinery around it. The senior staff, hard working and conscientious, was undoubtedly an asset to the Post Office, to remove them prematurely was a measure that did nothing by way of improving the quality of the job. The pace of change was dramatic and to some extent frightening, bringing with it uncertainty and stress.

Many of the senior workers were concerned about the sea change that affected the workplace but especially the flawed decisions that began to surface. Sometimes, not properly thought out ones came and went in rapid succession, leaving workers vague and uncertain. Machines that cost an enormous amount of money needed properly trained staff to manage them, yet it was the time when the recruitment policy changed considerably. Normal recruitment ceased, part time post persons were introduced; casual workers who were once only allowed at Christmas time – became standard procedure. We the regulars got the impression that the impact of three categories of workers created a conflict of interest. We were viewed with suspicion, partly because part timers thought we did not approve of them. Casuals felt we ill appreciated their presence and we the regulars felt that management paid too much attention to their new interest rather than us.

That conflict hampered the job to a large degree and ultimately affected morale. Many of us felt, perhaps justifiably – that the thoroughness and positive interest that we the senior post persons gave to the job, was not always matched by the new recruits. It would not be unreasonable to say that many of the part timers who had other interests outside of the Post Office did not have the same commitment that the regulars such as myself had. Many showed lack of concern. In the interim we felt management did not measure the impending problem adequately, even though there were monthly seminars. Subsequently those discussions became a mere talk shop ritual rather than a problem solving exercise.

One of the Post Office's great strength was the pulling together and the very collective way that work was carried out. It was a regime that depended largely on effort and co-operation from every level if it was to succeed. It was undoubtedly a lowly paid job and if there was a grey area, it was simply that postal workers were not properly rewarded for the wholesome effort that most of us gave to the job. What we enjoyed from management in my early years was a measure of goodwill and a degree of incentive that encouraged adequate responses. The Post Office enjoyed financial success for a number of years. It was without doubt a thriving organisation. What evolved subsequently was a scheme that lacked the initial training we were privileged to have. That training, in my opinion, gave us a valuable insight in understanding the function and in so doing helped the job along.

The change that came about brought a new management attitude. Some were more concerned with their own image and self-worth than what was relevant to good result. Incentives were removed, workers morale fell and the goodwill that prevailed for a number of years began to dwindle. That atmosphere of change was simply not conducive to proper development.

Just lately, we observed with some astonishment the failed name change, which resulted in nothing but embarrassment for the present management. Their attempt to remove a renowned and universally respected name like 'The Post Office' for the name 'Consignia', and then to spend £3 million to revert to the original name, truly indicates the lack of foresight of this new management.

It became quite clear to many of us that the early retirement policy, once established, was after all an opportunity to a life of relative freedom, away from the chores of full employment and the new prevailing attitude of management. For many it was an advantage worthy of consideration. My regret was that I was simply not able to accept the package. There was still much to be done in terms of family matters but more importantly, I was too far away from receiving a state pension. Nevertheless it was clear in my mind that any subsequent offer, once it was practical to do so, I would accept.

MOUNT PLEASANT
POSTAL OFFICE

It is ironical that much of my working life was spent in The Post Office – 'Mount Pleasant' and by the same token very little has been said about the place. To all intents and purposes, it was never my aim to work there for more than a limited period – three years – my entire focus was to amass a certain amount of cash, enough to take me to the United States for the important task of becoming an engineer. That was my agenda and it was only to this end that I was prepared to leave London Transport, no other reason.

Some years before I joined 'The Mount', I recall passing by the building – a huge unattractive place with a prison like appearance – and felt a sense of sympathy for the folks working there. I simply had no desire to be a member of that work force. It was sheer coincidence that I even remotely considered doing a spell there. An ex-colleague who worked on the Transport and with whom I made regular contact began showing me his pay packet and convinced me of the superior earnings that could be achieved, if I was mindful of doing so. We talked about our future plans and he assured me that the Mount was the ideal place to accrue quick and ready cash for what I had in mind. That of course fitted adequately to my scheme of things and as a result prompted my interest.

Since The Post Office was no longer a part of the Civil Service, the recruitment aspect had changed. The access to employment was less difficult than it had been, and at that period of time the wages were marginally superior to that of my present employment. Added to that, it was a period when shortage of staff dictated easy access to overtime – given a degree of momentum therefore, it seemed plausible that much could be gained – cash wise – in a relatively short time.

My job as a relief foreman took me to every part of the Northern Line, meeting people and making friends. Many of the people I met who were around my age group were equally keen to share those things of interest that helped to shape our social condition. Perhaps it would be fair to say that the quality of my life in terms of social interaction was better on the transport than that of the Post Office. It was an outdoor job, moving from place to place. Not so the Post Office which was of a different creation. The confined nature of my new job made it difficult for me to settle. The obvious truth was that I simply engaged in my own singular preoccupation of achieving my aim, which based on the circumstances around me, by now were becoming unachievable. It was almost twelve years before reality kicked in. With me getting older, it became a case of looking after my family – my wife was far from well and making sure that my children were adequately taken care of, equally important, making sure that all payments regarding my home were properly met.

Like it or not, the Post Office was now my job and it was up to me to make the best of what was available. With that in mind I made an honest effort to settle down to the task of working for a living. It suddenly became clear in my mind that I needed to subordinate my own personal ambitions for the sake of my loved ones, besides there was now a suspicion that my interest in ever becoming an engineer was beginning to wane. The redeeming feature of the job was that it offered a chance to earn much more by the way of overtime. That made it easy to attain any financial commitment far easier than would otherwise be the case. Very often it was time consuming, long and tiring. It has nevertheless served a very useful purpose and looking back it was a sacrifice that I have come to fully appreciate.

By far the most important aspect of my employment there, were the people I came in contact with. I became an active member of a club we formed – The Caribbean Social Society – which gave us fourteen years of social interaction and which was responsible for enriching our lives over those years. For me anyway, it was truly a remarkable experience, meeting, working and associating with people whose tremendous minds and personalities were exceptional. Out of those meetings I have developed friendships which helped to sustain me throughout my years there. Such people as Danny De Weaver, Felix Edwards, Vere Ward, Newton Peterson, Frankie Struthers, Lloyd Francis,

Des Dunes, Oliver DeVerney, Pat Irish, Larry Jones and Denis Morgan, to name but a few. Those men and the memories I shared with them would forever be treasured. Their wisdom and good sense that was on offer were perpetually inspiring. I shall always be grateful for knowing them.

MY THIRD VISIT TO
MY HOMELAND

I was approaching my sixtieth birthday, extremely tired and needing a rest. My wife and I decided to escape to the homeland for my last and most recent visit. Guyana too was under new management. The Peoples Progressive Party was now in office for their second term. The Opposition was at odds about the fairness of the election. There was a thick cloud of unpleasantness about the place and the excitement that I always manage to conjure up when there, soon subsided. The mood of the parties reflected widely across the country, leaving an undertone among the people that was most unsavoury. My village – a once very pleasant place to be – was now in a state that could only be considered as substandard. Georgetown, known as the Garden City was now a place that had lost its beauty and most of its charm.

Perhaps out of its post colonial history the years of unrest, the turmoil that the people have endured has to my mind highlighted a character change, which is alien to what I remembered as a young man. The generous and co-ordinated people have seemingly developed the propensity of taking and not giving back. We the older Guyanese have left a legacy worthy of mention. Our standards and discipline were exemplary. Guyanese workers were always in demand in both the Caribbean and the wider world. Our ability and professionalism made us a shining light of which few can deny. To watch a country such as ours stumble into oblivion is as remarkable as it is unfortunate. Our recovery can only begin if common sense prevails. We are now regarded as a political *'hot spot'*. The only option available for the eventual survival of the country is to mobilise the human resource available and work for the common good of all. Guyana cannot afford ethnic divide. We are on a flight to certain destruction if we do not pay attention to the enormous plight that the country happens to be in. It is therefore incumbent on the political power brokers to recognise the problems and to act swiftly to address them. They must lead by example or allow the country once the most respected in the Caribbean, to be regarded by all and sundry as a place for ridicule.

I returned in a state of anti-climax. What should have been a month of unrivalled joy; sadly was no more than a memory of ordinary proportions.

The pace that was set by the Post Office began to gather momentum. A package was on offer for early retirement and I was not about to refuse it. Those forty years that I have worked; those long hours that I endeavoured to do for the sake of my family was now coming to a glorious end. That, as fate would have it, was my lot. Regrets, I have a few. Perhaps I was never as ambitious as maybe I should have been. I did not have that little voice inside of me spurring me on. Maybe I gave up too easily or maybe my motivating machine was somewhat flawed. Whatever it was, I am grateful for my lot. I have a wonderful wife, three glorious kids and a grandson - all doing relatively well – and I enjoy a fair degree of good health. God I believe is watching over me and my family, what is more, I can tell at an instant as I look around, that there are many who are less fortunate than I am.

RETIREMENT

As I walked away from the chores and stresses of full time employment that October evening, I could not help feeling an overwhelming sense of freedom. For the first time in over forty years a new era had emerged. I was nevertheless mindful of the fact that the pay packet syndrome was at an end. I therefore needed to acquire new skills in the art of money management, especially since that particular commodity was now in short supply. However this was the time for new perspectives and challenges but most importantly it was a time to reflect; to reminisce about events that have gone before me. Events both personal and national which were undoubtedly part and parcel of my life's experiences; some of great significance, some not, but all of it has come to characterise the many changes – then and now - of that journey since my arrival in the United Kingdom.

* * *

I recall my very first visit to the doctor's surgery. It was my second week here and I was advised to register with a doctor. Doctor Beleg's surgery was relatively full and as I entered I indulged in that typical Guyanese habit – something that comes naturally - of greeting the folks therein with a bright and cheerful: "Good morning everyone!" The response was amazingly non-existent. With some embarrassment I quickly took my seat. It was refreshing to observe a woman who took the time to look up, smile sympathetically and resume her reading. It was clearly my first lesson of what not to do in a public place. That experience contrasted hugely with what I expected here in England. As I sat in a state of shock, Stayman came to mind. It was all too clear that my expectations as regards to the impeccable behaviour of the 'Englishman' as Stayman would have us believe, was severely dented in an instant. Their unwillingness to be courteous and to comply with basic manners as is common in the society from which I recently departed, left me in a state of bewilderment. First impressions count and since it was a completely new experience for me – it was hard to accept. It did occur to me as I sat in that unpleasant atmosphere, that accepting without question what people say as true or accurate can be a very dangerous pre-occupation.

Looking back, I can only conclude that I was a victim of Stayman's influence. He was of a mercurial nature and although I disliked his arrogance and pomposity, I was deeply fascinated by his great insight. He was an avid reader and was never backward in expounding his knowledge on most topics with clarity and authority. My impressionable mind such as it was, told me that he was always right but suddenly I came to realise that he had never travelled and much of what he said about the Englishman was not based in any way on experience. It was entirely a configuration of mind, a figment of his imagination and no more.

* * *

What would have been one of the most memorable occasions in London, without a doubt, was perhaps 'my first Saturday night on the town – in the West End.' To call it an obsession would be an exaggeration, but I recall having a compelling urge not only to see but also to experience my first ride on the underground. It became a major topic of conversation from the first day I arrived, mainly because it seemed so incomprehensible to imagine - the idea of a train deep in the bowels of the earth. As a result my curiosity to experience this fantastic feat of engineering got the better of me.

Trains were not new to me. The Guyana Transport Service, both on the East and West Coasts of Demerara, were not only efficient but also reliable. The thought of having such a huge contraption operating so deep underground mystified me. Since I was in the mode of 'seeing was believing', I needed to see and experience this phenomenon for myself. George, realising my alarming preoccupation with this subject, decided to give it optimum impact by adding a touch of mystery to the occasion. We travelled to our destination, Leicester Square by bus, and on arrival, we kicked off the evening with a pint of beer – it was warm as I recall, at the Porcupine Pub nearby. As we sipped our beer, the buzz that emanated from the Square gave me a sense of unbridled anticipation. The noise was deafening! It was as if everyone had something to say and it seemed that they were all saying it at the same time. The atmosphere was electric and even though I was enjoying my pint, I was over eager to join the multitude in this exceptional and interesting place.

The Square was full of amazing activities. I was impressed with the many cinemas, theatres, clubs, restaurants, and street entertainers - all in close proximity. We ate roasted chestnuts and Walls ice cream as we sauntered around the area with me taking in every activity with enormous interest. To say that I was not caught up with the general atmosphere of the evening would not be giving a true account of what I was experiencing, so much so, when George indicated that it was time for our homeward journey, I was just hoping that we would tarry a little longer. Up till then, I was preoccupied with the present surroundings and never gave much thought to what was next in store for me.

Our homeward journey led us to Piccadilly Circus and as I entering the circulating area, there before my very eyes was something I never saw – a moving stairway. George informed me that it was called an escalator, and as I held tightly to the rails of this moving item, descending towards the platform, I was now certain I was in the process of beholding a train that truly runs deep in the bowels of the earth.

The platform was full of revellers mostly returning home after a night out. It was obvious this was a big night for folks 'to let their hair down.' The newness of it all was a little overwhelming. Just then without warning I heard a crashing sound of a moving object coming towards me. As it got nearer, it became a roar, and sure enough this object materialised with a great rush and was now standing in the platform. My excitement was now complete as I was seeing an underground train for the first time, but as I entered and took a seat, it became clear to me that I was in the majority of one, since I was the only person on board with such feelings. This ride was no more than a routine exercise for the passengers on board. Many were reading the Evening News and Standard, some discussing football results or checking their pools' sheets. But mostly, all of it was on a casual level. None of it, however, could cull the excitement of a wonderful evening I had on the first Saturday night I spent in London, especially my maiden tube ride!

* * *

I remember getting lost in a thick blanket of smog. The year was 1962. Visibility was down to near zero, and traffic came to a halt. That evening on my way home, I was advised by my work colleagues to be careful. They said it was quite easy to get lost in the fog. I took the advice lightly since I regarded the possibility of me getting lost somewhat inconceivable. Much to my surprise, my complacency set me on a road to disaster. With my self-confidence high and my disregard for the prevailing conditions around me, I took the wrong turning and I found myself totally and comprehensively lost.

My wounded pride kept me from seeking assistance and after a while in what seemed like a futile gesture but more importantly, forced by desperation, I finally conceded and asked for assistance. It was a humiliating experience, one that I did not share too readily with my friends.

* * *

I recall the very early years in London, and how much we looked forward to visiting what was considered the most social institution in the land – the British pub. Television back then was a rare commodity and as a source of high atmosphere and good entertainment, the pub was the place to be. As young men, most of us found that a good pint went down a treat. Working as I did for Transport and the Post Office, it was regarded by my colleagues and myself as a very healthy social habit. Perhaps the confidence we derived from drinking as we did was matched by the amount of public lavatories that was in evidence day and night. Yes, London possessed an impressive array of toilets across the metropolis. Confidence to drink was high and even though we were young men with excellent retention qualities, there was always a 'loo' to ones disposal in case of need. Today sadly; and especially now that we are older and the necessity for them becomes greater, alas very few if any are available. Right now it is common practice to see people urinating around the city without a care in the world. That is of course a sad reflection on those with a civic duty to maintain a facility of such importance – not to mention restoring pride to older folks such as us. The city would undoubtedly benefit, even if it were only for the sake of decency and proper sanitation. London is a place with such an international profile; it can hardly afford to ignore a problem of such magnitude. What price having a wonderful progressive city smelling like the back end of a neglected pony? London has since acquired a greater number of drinking places over the years, in that same period the 'loo' has certainly become something of a rarity.

* * *

One of the memorable sights of London for many others and me was observing the ebb and flow of London's bowler-hat brigade. Without a doubt it was the most fascinating and original feature of the city. Unique with their dark suits folded umbrellas and brief cases; these civil servants epitomised power, authority and responsibility in a massive way and could easily have been an unusual tourist attraction. Unfortunately that fascinating scene has now disappeared. My high esteem subsided somewhat however when on platform duty one evening at the Bank station, I retrieved an article dropped from the pocket of one of these fine upstanding gentlemen, as he bent over to pick up his briefcase upon the arrival of a train. The package was quite heavy and as I offered it to the person concerned, he became flushed and agitated. "It's not mine. Nothing to do with me" He snapped as he hurried away to the far end of the platform.

Since I was more than certain that the package belonged to none other than the gentleman in question, I became suspicious. Sure enough my suspicions were vindicated. My bowler-hat friend was dealing in porn. The kind that could easily be taken seriously by the law and as a result could damage anyone's reputation if caught. It was a lesson learnt since I did not expect reputable men to indulge in matters so repugnant. Respectable pillars of society were never expected to shock us with such behaviour.

Leafy middle England, one imagined, was incapable of such lewd acts. It was a different era. Society was as discreet as it was closed and one wonders if the evil acts of crimes such as paedophiles, pornography and child abuse was any different from what it is today, or is this a new phenomenon which has invaded society? I would like to believe that the establishment of yesteryear was far more capable of keeping such awful matters under wraps.

* * *

Throughout my conscious life in school and much of my adolescent years, I have heard or read about Marylebone Cricket Club (MCC). It was therefore no great surprise that it was high on my agenda of places to visit on my arrival here. Ironically, although I liked and supported Surrey as a youth, I always regarded Lords as a very special place.

It was a delightful morning and I was brimful of excitement as I entered through the gates of this great and wonderful sport.

My thrill was truly compounded by the fact that Sir Garfield Sobers-the finest cricketer of my time- was playing for Nottingham against Middlesex. That of course added to the general aura of the occasion. I must admit that I was completely and utterly smitten!

As I walked across this hallowed ground, I found myself looking for trees, but there was none. How different it was to our own National stadium, Bourda, in Guyana and it was so much bigger.

I took my seat and anxiously waited for the match to commence and with time on my hands, my thoughts drifted back to Bourda and the first test match that I saw there, which as it happened turned out to be quite funny and somewhat bizarre experience.

I had saved enough money to watch my first test match between India and the West Indies. It was certainly not an everyday occurrence at that time. Going to town to watch test cricket was a very serious business indeed.

That morning was an exceptional one for me. I literally arrived in Georgetown at least three hours before the actual game and for some strange and unknown reason, I decided to ride around the city merely to waste a bit of time.

Riding down Regent Street I saw a gathering. It was a small crowd of men behaving in a somewhat excitable manner. Curiosity took the better of me, so I stopped. They were playing a strange game that I had never seen before. It was called 'Find the lady', better known as 'three cards'. The accomplice - always looking for new mugs like myself - started encouraging me to have a go. He told me he was losing and if I could find the lady, he would be most grateful. After successfully finding the lady on a few occasions, he then persuaded me to play for cash since I was so lucky. What happened next was an utter and complete blur. In a remarkably short time, I managed to rid myself of all the money I possessed. I was broke and was now in a state of complete shock, especially realising that the opportunity of watching the test which I had long anticipated had now gone.

In this totally disconsolate state, I kept asking myself, what would I tell the folks back home. How could I be so naïve to fall for such a silly stunt?

I began my homeward journey numb to the core. Oblivious of anyone or anything, searching my mind for something tangible to tell the folks when I returned home. One thing was certain, it was far too embarrassing to tell the truth.

I was half way home when I saw a villager waving frantically at me. He was riding into town to watch the game, but had no plans to pay for the privilege. His intention was to watch the game from one of the trees around Bourda. He assured me that it was good fun and began encouraging me to accompany him.

Lloyd's exuberance of spirit made him a very likeable individual and very often his persuasive habit becomes infectious. "Come on" he said, "why pay for something that you could get for free? ... and besides, you can see the game as well as anyone from up there."

Up till then it never occurred to me that watching cricket from high up a tree was an option I would have considered. To be preferably honest, I was not overtly sold on the idea, but the fact that I was financially stranded and this seemed an easy way out of my present predicament, I reluctantly agreed to Lloyd's request.

Since we were early, we managed to secure adequate viewing points. Me, high up on a limb: Lloyd immediately below me. It was a spectacular sight up there. Excellent viewing to say the least. It would also be true to say however; that if there was a grey area to this new venture of mine, it was sitting up a tree for long hours. It presents a very serious problem to one's posterior. For someone like me who is devoid of flesh in that department, it was not fun. It was simply an endurance test.

I watched Everton Weeks and Clyde Walcott batting against the great Indian spinner Gupti and wondered how these professionals were able to make the game of cricket look so ridiculously easy. They were building a good partnership and I was totally immersed in the proceedings, when I was distracted by a loud shout. It was just before lunch and it was coming from under the tree. What was more, this person was directing his call to me.

"You up there, with the cream shirt and brown pants". I looked down only to find him looking directly at me. "Yes you" he said, "Your sitting on my limb and I am coming up you have one minute to get down or I'm coming up to throw you off! " He obviously picked on me because of my size. With such a menacing attitude, this stranger seemed the type that would do anything to get his own way. I immediately decided, in the best interest of safety (my own), I would heed this man's aggressive intent. Lloyd, who was sitting immediately under me, stood up. "Vic" he said " You sit right where you are and let me see the man that would remove you".

Silence descended upon the tree. My instinct told me to vacate the limb as quickly as possible. But that would have surely undermined my good friend's authority. The stranger stopped his climb and directed his fearful gaze at Lloyd. "Do you think you can scare me? The man asked, "Are you man enough to stop me? He continued. Lloyd's glare became just as ferocious as this upstart. "You lay a finger on him and you will know who is man from boy" informed Lloyd.

The stranger stopped in his tracks. I was utterly stunned; Lloyd was someone of about six foot in height, stout of chest and sturdy built. But whatever he was, he was not a warrior. In fact, if the truth is to be told, he was no more than a coward. He was a gentle giant, who kept well away from any kind of conflict. In the village, he was renowned for his dancing. We called him the king of "Bop". His elegance on the dance floor was stunning, his footwork majestic. Fighting or challenging people was not his forte.

However, here he was defending me and I was not about to let him down. His booming voice and sturdy chest were impressive credentials. It was certainly those assets that made this stranger retreat. Leaving me to watch my game in relative peace.

Needless to say, that was my first and last trip up the famous Bourda trees. On our way home I asked Lloyd what would have happened if this horrible man had decided to climb the tree? He would only laugh and kept on saying "I disarmed him, I called his bluff and that is all that mattered". In the end he was right, it was all that mattered. However, in my estimation, Lloyd was playing a very dangerous game indeed and it certainly was not cricket. Incidentally, watching the gentlemen's game at Lord's carried no risk. It was a relaxing and serene occasion and Sir Gary Sobers, as expected, displayed excellence of the highest calibre. It was sure enough a very exciting day's cricket.

* * *

One of the greatest features of London City was its large array of hospitals. Unfortunately that has become another casualty (no pun intended) in the scheme of things. The hospitals in the early years of my life here were well-run and totally reliable intuitions. The pride and purpose of the matron was visible evidence of competence, efficiency and responsibility combined, which was part and parcel of their job. Driven by discipline, enthusiasm and the desire to please, matrons ran a tight ship. Hospitals were neat, tidy and hygienic places. Matrons saw to that. Nurses did their work, more as a vocation – especially since they were poorly paid – and patients felt safe in their hands. Strict adherence to hospital rules was apparent. Nurses were never allowed to wear their uniform on the street. Special shoes were worn and generally standards were excellent.

It is difficult to understand the wisdom of replacing matrons for managers; whose interest and agenda were poles apart. Matron's interests are in patients, managers are target setters. Without a doubt matrons were the natural embodiment of the caring system. Long years of training, acquiring skills, and with the ability to understand how the system functioned, made them irreplaceable.

It is interesting to note that many of the nurses were recruits from the Caribbean, filling a void that existed at that time. Thanks to Enoch Powell who was responsible for bringing them here.

Our young student nurses worked their way through the system, in what was very often in difficult times and trying circumstances to become good nurses, midwives and matrons themselves. No one can deny the mammoth contribution our girls have made in their endeavour to give satisfaction to a worthwhile career. Many have reached the age of retirement after more than four decades, leaving a vacuum to be filled once more. Set against today's trend where beds are short, waiting lists are long, patients are dying on trolleys and cross infection is prevalent, it would take a super optimist to predict the hospital's future. Unfortunately it is at a time when demand is greater than ever, when people are living longer and patients are older, yet it is exactly when hospitals are less likely to cope.

* * *

I remember vividly an incident mainly for its impact on me many years ago. I was only a few short months as a foreman and I was scheduled to open Hampstead when my alarm failed to go off one morning. In a state of panic, I was up and out, basically hoping for a miracle. I had forty minutes to get there, and Hampstead being an important station, I felt an urgent need to be there in time. Still running, I reached Seven Sisters Road as I observed a motorcyclist slowing – then stopped. My first thought was that it was someone who knew me. A Godsend – but it turned out to be a complete stranger. He enquired where I was going and offered to take me to Chalk Farm. I accepted readily, he was the owner of a brand new Triumph – a most beautiful and well-made machine. So impressed was I that I could not help commenting about his superb machine. Not only was he keen to talk about this fine vehicle, he went on to express the superiority of his country's manufacturing might. He spoke of the Norton and the Matchless as machines of excellence and was boastful of his own engineering skills. He was not slow in informing me that the technical training – including apprenticeship in this country was second to none and even though I found some of his comments somewhat abrasive, I could not help agreeing tacitly that he was correct. I recall being the proud owner of my first bicycle – a Raleigh - at eighteen. What pleasure it gave me. My friend Fitzroy had a *Rudge*, Danny owned a

Humber. We argued incessantly about which of these three machines - all British made – were superior, and marvelled at the workmanship of those delightful machines. Our railways, cars, trucks, lorries, radios and many other utilities were all made in Great Britain. It was a taken for granted feature of this country. Today Briton has abandoned its manufacturing base to places like Japan and Germany to mention a few. An amazing exodus of trained people has gone abroad merely to keep their skills alive. Traditional apprenticeship has also disappeared. One cannot help thinking that such a colossal loss in any society must have a detrimental effect on the economy of this or any other country.

* * *

My first week here was memorable for many reasons. It was a week when many things were told to me that did not immediately make sense. For instance, George told me that it was alright to wash in the basement while it was warm but in the winter washing there was out of bounds, so I would have to use the public baths. In order not to appear totally naïve I shook my head in agreement. Since George was a level-headed sort of chap and I respected his sanity, I felt he knew what he was saying - but why should I or anyone want to have a wash in public? He must have seen how puzzled I was so he decided that very weekend to put me out of my misery. Bright and early on the first Saturday morning here, I was taken to Hornsey public baths. It was quite an experience. Never before have I seen so many people standing in a queue waiting to have a wash. This was strictly a weekend affair; a British tradition which lasted for many years. It was brought home to me most vividly when I was house hunting only to find many of the average homes were without bathrooms. Coming from the tropics I found that to be an extremely strange habit.

* * *

Another thing that springs to mind was the morning I took a casual walk to Holloway Road 'Nag's Head'. I believe it was my third morning in London. Across the way I saw this shop that had a familiar look to it. Could it be what I thought it was? I quickly entered the building expecting it to be none other than a Caribbean style 'cake shop' but on going in I realised the similarity ended abruptly. The place was nothing more than a newsagent. The morning was warm and I was hoping to make a purchase of something cold and fizzy to quench my thirst but there was no such thing on offer. The old fellow behind the counter asked me what I wanted. Without hesitation I said, "A cold drink". He looked at me in a most bewildered fashion.

"A cold drink?" he echoed. "This is a newsagent, mate." I looked up on the shelf and saw a few bottles of Tizer that seemed to have been there for a long time. The old fellow followed my vision and in a quizzical manner he asked. "Do you want one of these?" I could see he was enjoying himself at my expense.

"No," I said, "If it's not cold". I did not wait for a reply because I knew instantly I had made a fool of myself. Why should I expect to find 'cake shops' in England? I was many miles away from home. I was living in London now and such things were not peculiar to this environment. Interestingly though, it brings a smile to my face to know that I can now purchase a cold drink from a newsagent.

* * *

I remember the introduction of the Race Relations Board. It was a statute that was designed to remove the abuse and other practices that were distinctly disadvantageous to the ethnic minorities. Unfortunately, its limited powers rendered it somewhat impotent - although to be fair it succeeded among other things, to remove the hideous 'No Irish, no coloureds, no dogs' signs from public view.

* * *

I recall Enoch Powell's 'Rivers of blood' speech and wondered why a man who was considered by many as thoroughly decent, and who was primarily responsible for the recruitment of Caribbean people to these shores found it necessary to sully his good name. By so doing – it is my considered opinion that it was merely for political expediency; to raise his stake in the arena of power, more than a squalid piece of mischief making. Whatever it was, it certainly was not an act of harmony or goodwill, nor did it enhance his status in the eyes and hearts of decent law-abiding people – especially ethnic minorities – who expect better from men in public office.

* * *

I recall Ted Heath's three-day week with much clamour from bosses to curb the union's abuse of power. That power was eroded by the Conservative government's free market theory. Under Maggie Thatcher's rule, the boot was firmly on the other foot. Bosses were now in control; hire and fire took centre stage. Workers' rights were trampled in the dust; 'job for life' became a distant memory. Part timers and agencies ruled, OK! And much of what was achieved by way of improvement over many years began to slip into reverse. Even pensions that were once as safe as houses were under threat. The end result was inevitable; workers became vulnerable, leaving fear and stress in its wake. How amazing to see the pendulums swinging full circle. Bosses were awarding themselves large bonuses irrespective of success or failure – golden handshake if you win or loose, not to forget pensions of great magnitude. Some might say that was abuse on a very grand scale.

* * *

I remember the emergence of Maggie Thatcher, the first woman Prime Minister and leader of the Conservative Government. That period heralded an important philosophical shift from the British way of life. Traditional politics disappeared. Daring and controversial policies became the norm. Maggie's weird and not so wonderful political cocktail affected a multitude of people – bringing untold misery as a result. In her pursuit to establish her own brand of political idealism, 'The Iron Lady' as she was known, discarded the old established order for a new way. Nothing was sacrosanct.

Her first venture was the sale of Council houses – which ironically was seen by many as a popular measure. That policy removed at an instant, the old culture of renting, thereby making home ownership an attractive alternative. It also provided a springboard for the government to pursue measures that were far-reaching and most unpopular across the political spectrum. Privatisation reigned supreme, hospitals were closed, matrons were phased out in place came managers who themselves became target setters. Under a strict budget system operations were done within the limits of cash given. It became an obvious case of no money no operations until the next budget. Councils were capped, limiting their spending. Cleaning, (hospitals included) were contracted out for the most part taking away the 'in house' responsibility of companies achieving good standard hygiene. Little wonder, patients were going into hospitals with an illness, only to leave with cross infections such as M.R.S.A. Mental Institutions and Hostels were closed, the abandonment of The Greater London Council, the disenfranchisement of unions in having an influence in matters relating to government. Not only were the rules changed by statute to weaken the power of unions, the government presided over strikes from the printers, the dockers but more especially, the miners; a prolonged strike that lasted for over a year. Unemployment, regarded as a serious political issue soared to over four million.

The industrial base, the country's main pillar for development was seriously hampered, ripping apart families and setting a unique precedence of uncertainty and vulnerability to many millions in its wake. By far the most emotive issue however, was the dreaded poll tax. It was a policy too far and for once the 'Iron Lady' who incidentally was not for turning, relented. Forced by a reaction of hostility not seen in this land for many a year, the policy was rescinded.

The problem that was born out of that era was a direct result of a government which showed a callous disregard for society, cared very little for foreigners, despised trade unions, hated socialism and simply abhorred collective consensus. The working class was only useful at election time. Maggie's office did nothing to enhance her own gender in 1974 when she said: *"It will be years and not in my lifetime before a woman becomes Prime Minister"*. It was a sentiment which typified the person she was and which smacks on selfishness. It surely is part of an unfortunate legacy that she left behind.

* * *

I remember that awful January evening of 1981 when tragedy struck New Cross. A house fire started mysteriously, killing thirteen teenage kids enjoying themselves at a house party. No one was ever held to account. It is unimaginable the pain and grief those unfortunate parents endured on that wretched evening and for the rest of their lives knowing that never again would they see their loved ones. The emotions of that evening were shared by all of us. It was an experience that was unmatched for the horror and misery it brought to the lives of so many. How or why did it ever happen? We shall never know. The speculation was endless. It ranged from a racist attack to an incident or accident within. Those responsible for bringing justice, namely, the police, did not cover themselves with glory in finding who was responsible.

* * *

I remember the brutal and vicious attack on Stephen Lawrence in 1993. Killed by racist thugs when all he was doing was trying to be a decent human being with expectations of growing up and achieving his full potential in a neutral and civilised environment. It is something that decent law abiding people strive for. Stephen, alas, did not have that opportunity; cut down by mindless morons whose only sense of purpose was to be destructive; who all but bragged about their evil-doing and got away with it. Again those responsible for bringing justice, namely, the police, did not bring anyone to book.

* * *

Just recently, at the beginning of the new Millennium, November 2000, a young schoolboy, Damilolo Taylor, a ten-year-old, died in tragic circumstances on a stairwell in North Peckham. It took six years for the police to apprehend the culprits who ended the life of a charming, clever young lad. The emptiness and frustration of those who have lost their loved ones, and whose pain and anguish is compounded by the fact that it had taken so long for someone to be held accountable for such acts, is very real.

Those three incidents- and there are many more – have clearly stamped their footprint on the environment – the society and especially, the Justice system. The question that is constantly asked is: *'Do the police use their energy and resources to its optimum when they are dealing with matters concerning visible minorities?'* Britain is a country where the police have sophisticated forms of detection and surveillance, where information gathering is at an advanced level. Solving crimes is achieved more and more by scientific methods; it is extraordinary that the ethnic minority is less satisfied with the treatment of the law than should otherwise be the case.

Law enforcement is fundamental to every decent and civilised society. Great Britain has been a nation proud of its history in terms of fair play and justice for all. Yet many of us who have lived in the society for half a century (some longer), have developed a sense of cynicism for the way the law enforcement machinery operates towards us. What we seek is a system that gives the same measure of justice for all its citizens irrespective of their colour. Yet the converse is true. Statistics have revealed a steady and consistent bias towards people of colour. The police are far more likely to apprehend black folks in greater numbers; the magistracy and Judges still see good reason to incarcerate our young men as opposed to their white contemporaries. There still exists an imbalance that hardly leaves us satisfied; a feeling that causes distrust and bewilderment and leaves us with the presumption that the post colonial residue of ill regard for our people is still very much intact. The two incidents that spring readily to mind were the Brixton Riots in 1981 and the Broadwater Farm disturbances in October 1985. Racial tension was high as a result of police harassment and there was a sense of inevitability of that incoming disaster. The indignity of Stop and search; 'Operation Swamp', especially among African Caribbean's – not to mention other atrocities like verbal abuse that were primarily responsible for the riot.

It fuelled an already vulnerable situation and the astonishing degree of insensitivity that was shown by the law enforcers only compounded the very obvious problem that existed at the time. It was as if they were inviting confrontation when what was needed was a measure of common sense and constructive policing.

The Broadwater Farm riot of October 1985 was precipitated by the death of Cynthia Jarret during a police raid on her home. Once again their aggressive intent was very much in evidence. It was an incident that did nothing for good public relations. Police harassment versus a volatile crowd, created the basis of an explosion that was ultimately responsible for the death of policeman Keith Blakelock. However, the problem cannot be placed on the police alone. It was the government of the day who showed a remarkable lack of political will which caused an amazingly awful situation to deteriorate further. Discrimination by and large was responsible for what happened that day and is still happening today. It is fatuous to believe that matters such as this can be left to the police and a moderate degree of community work to solve a problem as intractable as this. Racism and discrimination are deeply rooted in the fabric of this society. It cannot be treated as if it is an apparition; it requires a serious and very conscious effort from every walk of life but especially the government whose good example would have a transient power on society's rank and file. We the ethnic minority need to have faith in the society that we live in. We must feel comfortable in the environment that happens to be our home for many years. To be targeted by any section of society merely for being visible, should not be tolerated. Institutional racism as illustrated by the McPherson enquiry needs vigorous attention.

The case of ex-paratrooper Christopher Alder, who was choking in his own blood, while police stood and watched, when prompt attention was necessary. Yet another example was the offensive behaviour towards Sam Farquharson – who was maltreated, called a black bastard, a coon and had his shoe tied to his trousers because coons have tails, was far from acceptable.

Efforts must be made to have a standard criterion working for all its citizens, thereby giving greater confidence to the ethnic minorities. Greater co-operation would undoubtedly result if people were aware that the law is not working with an unfair bias against them. We have more than served our probation. Many of us have given our youth and much of our maturity to this country. We are living in a multicultural society. Once again let me reiterate; any government with the vision and the propensity for change must undoubtedly make a huge difference. We patiently await such good intentions.

* * *

I vividly remembered waking up in absolute consternation on 31st August 1997 to the news that Princess Diana, the Princess of Wales had died in a road accident. The shock of that news resonated in my system for what seemed like eternity and left me numb with disbelief. My family and I were holidaying in Italy. It was our first visit to that Country and just four days before we took a boat trip to Porto Fino and discovered the yacht belonging to Jody where the Princess was on holiday, moored just outside the island. As we went by the buzz of excitement was electric. Everyone wanted to catch a glimpse of her but unfortunately she was not in public view. Although we were all disappointed at not seeing her, much of the topic in our midst was related to or about her.

To have died so young - so prematurely was as calamitous as it was sad. The Princess personified excellence, with an amazing penchant for getting things done. Her unselfish humanitarian spirit was very much in evidence. Always pro-active and sometimes beyond the call of duty, she constantly raised awareness of society's ills both here and in the wider world. Her acts of goodwill will be etched in the hearts of many and she would always be remembered for her kindness and her humility.

* * *

The greatest political surprise I can recall was the collapse of communism and the eventual end of the cold war. Although much was said about the world being a better place without it, I stand firmly with those who have great reservations to the contrary. My concerns and that of so many are that such an act only proceeds to create an imbalance in the World power structure. History has shown that such power can ultimately lead to intimidation, coercion, destitution and abuse.

The world is threatened by a new phenomenon that is terrorism. It is as dangerous as it is destructive and it can raise its ugly head anytime, anywhere – as was seen in the United States on the 11th September; destroying the lives of so many innocent people. Terrorism is insidious by its very nature and should be challenged, not by force but by a more intellectual approach. That option has a greater possibility of success in winning hearts and minds than any kind of hostility. Rich countries can begin by removing squalor, oppression, hunger and inequality wherever it exists and perhaps this universe of ours can be a much better place for all mankind.

* * *

Perhaps the greatest and immediate impact on my arrival in London was to behold a white beggar on the streets on my first day. Such things I imagined only belong to countries such as the one I left behind. Never could I have imagined such a spectacle in a city such as London.

* * *

The Liberals it was said had hardly enough Members of Parliament to fit into one taxi. Today now known as The Liberal Democrats, the membership of the party has increased more than ten fold. In our ever-changing world, who know what will happen in the future for this party? They may possibly become the Official Opposition of the country in the not too distant future.

* * *

The milkman and his dairy product was perhaps the most conspicuous of the community as I recall. But the strange and unusual habit of leaving bread unwrapped and exposed on residents' doorsteps was a most surprising oddity to most Caribbean nationals. The emergence of the supermarket has almost completely extinguished that culture.

* * *

I remember – with pleasant fondness – Lyons Corner House not only for its original tea scones and crumble, but also because it was a major source of employment for many immigrants, especially students and professionals who could not find suitable or immediate employment elsewhere.

* * *

My greatest political satisfaction was to see the release of Nelson Mandela after he had spent twenty-seven years in South Africa's penal institution on Robben Island. Not only did he emerge as leader and head of government four years later but also he succeeded in removing the odious and abominable spectre of apartheid. Here is an outstanding human being who believes in the principle of justice, equality and fair play. The apartheid regime was the last vestige of a system that is remembered for its vile and inhuman oppression of millions of Africans – while the developed world sat tacitly and did not lift a finger to eliminate this evil act. Nelson's bravery, his defiance and amazing resilience stood the test of time. In the face of adversity and imminent danger he stood with iron will and unbending courage, not only to overcome but also to triumph against impossible odds and to lead his people out of an unsavoury and hostile hate-ridden regime. With the help of Winnie Mandela who worked assiduously and contributed in no uncertain manner to remove the scourge that engulfed South Africa's people for so long.

If achieving the highest office of President was not enough; Nelson showed magnanimity of the highest possible degree in forgiving those who were responsible for inflicting pain, torture, cruelty and death to so many. He is a consummate human being. His legacy is legendary and a wonderful example to mankind. Nelson Mandela is without doubt a great man and a true humanitarian.

* * *

Muhammad Ali was: extraordinary, irritating, outrageous, funny, fabulous, incredible, charming, confident and brilliant. Yes! He was all of those things to a multitude of people who loved and adored him. In his heyday he would "Float like a butterfly and sting like a bee". To my mind, perhaps he is one of the greatest athletes I can recall. When Muhammad won the Olympic gold medal, he told the world he would be the greatest champion ever. Very few would disagree that he was the remarkable fighting machine he so readily boasted about.

His fiercest battle anyway was against the establishment for doubting his sincerity and belief when he refused to be inducted into the army. He was pilloried, called a draft dodger, a felon and worse. However, he was never deterred. He remained resolute and never wavered. He showed the same level of dexterity in or out of the ring. A proud man, he ignored those who considered him uneducated, yet he spoke with wisdom and clarity far greater than those who professed to be scholars.

He was a boxer of immense ability. He feared no one and gave the world tremendous pleasure. His flamboyance was not always appreciated and there were a few who wished ill of him but Muhammad the man, the entertainer, the showman was a true icon and the memory of his wonderful skills will burn brightly in my memory forever.

* * *

The contentious debate and major controversy over asylum seekers seems to have a familiar ring to it. Three decades ago, we were right there – with bells ringing in our ears about our presence. 'Swamp' and 'enough is enough' was the theme, and the media, (especially the tabloids) who were never over enthusiastic in giving us favourable press, were having a field day about us changing the culture of this green and pleasant land.

The problem of asylum seekers is not one I am prepared to involve myself with. Genuine people have a legitimate right to stay, and the task to differentiate between honest and genuine seekers and the rest is difficult as it is without interference from any quarter. It is however, still fresh in the minds of so many Caribbean people, who, although we were invited to help with the tasks that no one else wanted to do, such as the railways, the tubes (underground), the buses the Post Office and the hospitals and here I must express the highest praise for our nurses who have endured racial intolerance and much abuse to ultimately triumph in their professional field, giving sterling effort throughout the years as nurses, midwives and matrons.

As for the rest of us, we managed to maintain and to bring stability to the various areas of employment that we were assigned to and now many of us are coming to the end of our working lives we must hope that those that are seeking entry would be able to fill the void that remains by our absence.

It is quite obvious to me, that people everywhere seeing and hearing about the prospects and opportunities of developed countries and the great benefits they can derive from being here, are seeking entry merely to advance their own cause. Many of these countries are less successful, and it is a natural human instinct to seek greener pastures. However, in the not too distant future, these new people would be quite able to assimilate into the society, leaving the visible minority to take the heat once more.

* * *

Two of the most illustrious and charismatic African American sons of the 20th century were undoubtedly Malcolm X and Dr Martin Luther King. Superlatives are hardly adequate to describe the human qualities – the incredible will and the undaunted devotion to duty they possessed in creating a historic path and a whole new way for the disadvantaged African Americans, by transforming the political process necessary for the advancement and fulfilment of its people across the entire spectrum of that society but more especially in the Deep South.

In their own different ways they were able to engender awareness to millions. The injustices that prevailed in a society that preached freedom and democracy but which was only too willing to deny people of colour, basic rights; a people who toiled relentlessly and gave their blood, sweat and tears to help build that country.

Born Malcolm Little, his early ambition was to become a lawyer but was discouraged from doing so by his white teacher who indicated to him that such a profession was strictly a preserve of whites and 'Negroes' should not have such high aspirations.

A sensitive young man by nature, who encountered racism in his homeland, fell victim and soon drifted into a world of wrong doings and crime, which got him imprisoned. It was there that his life took a significant change. He became a Muslim. His un-quenching desire for knowledge and his supreme understanding of the imbalance that the society embraced made him the most vocal and controversial activist in the United States. He was never afraid to challenge the injustices of the society. He was renowned for his militancy and believed in the principle of preaching and expounding the politics of discrimination. Never one to mince his words, The Muslim minister aggressively charged the society of letting down the very people that were instrument to their development and deplored their bigotry and ignorance where ever it existed.

The consciousness he highlighted brought to the fore of millions, his strong influence for change. A price that he paid for with his life, but his indomitable spirit and his unflinching philosophy has brought new energy and purpose to his people who needed someone of his calibre and stature to inspire confidence and to remove oppression from their midst. He fought and died for a worthy cause. He was a giant among men. His spirit would forever live on.

* * *

Doctor Martin Luther King was majestic as his name suggests. His bravery, his iron will, his affinity for his people and his belief in social equilibrium were both unequalled and un-quenching. His amazing chemistry of vision, intellect and eloquence made him a unique force and an outstanding leader of men. His great attributes as a debater and a skilled orator not only made him larger than life, he was perhaps the most 'listened to' and respected personality of his time.

A man of immense humility, he was always prepared to render his own personal safety for the common good of his people and regarded the 'love of life' as secondary to fulfilling his task of changing the face of society.

His influence in a country that was unwilling and somewhat determined to maintain their hold on keeping 'Negroes' in their place changed the face of history and restored much dignity to a people that suffered un-relentless indignity for many, many years.

His pursuit to give the African American their just reward made him a Goliath among men.

He was no ordinary mortal; he led by example and never deviated from the stated purpose of changing hearts and minds. They were those who despised him but could not help respecting his ability and human endeavour to withstand the tribulations and adversities that were synonymous with the struggle.

He preached non-violence and never deviated from his strong principle of changing society by peaceful means, and a great measure of success was ultimately achieved.

Doctor King's philosophy transcended all races. That he persuaded the bigots and the racist to examine their consciences, and to shame them into thinking objectively, was never in doubt. His remarkable ability to reach out to the most hardened and unwavering minority whose creed was welded in hate and destruction has been well documented. His clarity of thought can only be matched by his determination to create a sea change of attitudes across the whole spectrum of that vast country.

His star still shines brightly, illuminating us all in a hope that this world of ours can be guided by decency, morality and kindness and they can have greater merit than jealousy, envy and hate.

The names of Malcolm X and Doctor Martin Luther King still burn brightly in our hearts. Long may that memory last!

FINAL REVIEW

Now that I have reflected and tried to rekindle some of the events and experiences that mirrored the passage of my life, let me conclude that the journey was never lacking in endeavour or spirit. Much of it was a learning curve and although I hit the rocks from time to time, my resilience and the support that was at my disposal in so many ways, gave me the courage to carry on. My principles which I treasure dearly got in the way of what was regarded as progress but at no time was I prepared to compromise these qualities for promotion or gains. To that end, much of the experience that I have gained fills me with a degree of satisfaction. The golden rule that I have learnt, is that life is a battle that we all have to face and it is not fought in an arena of dreams. Things are not always what they appear to be. Many of the thoughts that engulfed me as a youth were not welded in reality but by boundless and youthful exuberance. The belief that success was just a matter of time – that all things were possible – that achieving goals was a simple or automatic exercise, were all part of that romantic notion that so many young minds are guilty of. For instance, what ever possessed us (and there were many) of Caribbean heritage to believe that going abroad, achieving great rewards and returning to our respective areas within five to ten years was possible? Why did we believe that success could be achieved by simply going abroad?

I recall how quickly I was shaken out of my complacency on my arrival here in London. Only a few short weeks ago I had the comfort of my Mum's home cooking. I was always spick and span. She made sure that was always the case. I was in a zone of relative ease, once I was under her care. On arrival, there were tasks that I was confronted with that challenged my competence in a very extreme way. It became clear to me also that the bachelor existence, which I so cherished, was in sharp contrast to what I enjoyed at home. I quickly realised that there was an urgent need for a woman's touch around me. My very first winter told me all I wanted to know about my status as a single man. Perhaps it was something to do with those long winter nights and very cold beds. Whatever it was, I was more than prepared to sacrifice the great and glorious position of bachelorhood for that of a married man. Once married, the task of working for a living and creating a family took priority over all else. In that great struggle for survival, those five or ten years simply vanish into obscurity.

My friend Elan is now firmly entrenched in Guyana once more. His personal ambition and ultimate dream, has always been to return to his homeland and his focus and determination has paid dividends. Elan acquired a substantial amount of real estate some years ago and on his return, built an attractive home that he now resides in. It is still my belief that had life played him a more favourable hand, things may have been different. He was unfortunate to have lost Megan (his wife died suddenly) so early in their marriage. The emotional impact of that loss was far reaching and in my opinion created a personality change of substantial magnitude. Although we remained friends, it was never as robust as it once was. He eventually migrated to Canada for a period before returning to his homeland.

Our discussion on the question of returning to Guyana was fairly extensive. He disclosed to me that an elaborate degree of mental and physical energy is needed to affect a smooth and successful return. It is a decision of primary importance that needs very serious thought and should not be taken lightly.

Guyana still looms largely in my thoughts. I still get an emotional high about the place and my patriotic zeal is not yet in short supply. When I am there, I feel a certain compatibility with the environment that would be difficult to surpass and it constantly reminds me of an experience I had when I was seventeen years old. An old friend, Stanley Cummings and I were leaving the plantation (Ogle sugar estate) one evening when we saw an old overseer returning from the cane fields. Harold Mitchell seemed older than his years. Perhaps that was due to the tropical sun beating down on him constantly. He was of retiring age and rumours of his departure were everywhere. He was someone of a pleasant demeanour and always seemed approachable. As he rode by, Stanley called out to him – hardly expecting him to engage us in proper conversation.

"Mr Mitchell, I hear you are retiring and going back to England." Stanley remarked. Mitchell smiled, nodded in the affirmative and carried on – then suddenly he stopped and turned his horse around to face us. "You are perfectly correct Laddie," he informed. "I am going back – but not to England. I belong to Edinburgh and that's where I am going". I thought it strange that he made the distinction. England as far as I was concerned, covered the whole geographical area. "What's the difference?" I asked.

Harold Mitchell laughed out aloud. "Laddie I am a Scotchman – not an Englishman". He said. "I have been away from my home for almost fifty years but my links with Scotland would never, ever diminish. It is where I was born and it is where I hope to rest my weary head". We watched him go and although his remarks about the homeland meant nothing then, I have learnt fully to appreciate the significance of that statement now. Perhaps consciously or unconsciously, that link with the place of our birth can never be truly diminished.

We have come to a point in our lives where many of us are now retired or about to do so, and feel the need to return to our homeland. That decision, whichever way the pendulum swings, has a great deal of merit to it. Those who are returning must not be motivated only by sentiment and emotion but by a deep commitment and a desire to do so. It is unquestionably a goal fulfilled. Particularly, the same is certainly true for those who are desirous of remaining. The effort, dedication and stout contribution that has been achieved over many years is enough justification for so doing. Mixed marriages and inter-island marriages can be a contentious issue, and problems can arise, but they are not insurmountable. All things are possible – subject to what we are comfortable with.

However it pans out anyway, we must now concentrate on giving what remains of our lives, the quality and purpose it deserves.

We have observed with great interest; the changing pace and times that have occurred. When we entered this society, everything seemed grey; today the colour is very much rainbow. Yes, multiculturalism is alive and well. The style and flair which was not in evidence when we arrived has not only been maintained but has gathered pace.

Our children are now adults and have children of their own. That we have made a path to which they can benefit – and a momentum for them to succeed, where many of us have failed, cannot be overstated. My fervent hope is that they use every opportunity that society offers in their best interest. They must be constructive, they must follow good example and to have a positive approach. These are some of the requirements that are needed to establish a purposeful existence. Those qualities no doubt will help them to reap rich rewards by their accomplishment and that would give us all great pride and much satisfaction.

It must be emphasised that we have not yet won a victory. The tide is changing but we are still a long way from winning the battle. The recently published statistics that Caribbean children are failing (mainly boys) speak volumes of the huge difficulties we are still confronted with. What is conspicuous and most disheartening about this problem, is the awareness of the education authorities, who since 1977 have full knowledge of this appalling situation and have done very little to correct it. As usual, promises to alter this unfortunate situation have resulted in failure.

The political party to which many of us affiliate and believe that it is the natural party to vote for, has not lived up to its expectations. Bold measures on their part to improve or to advance our cause, is not politically expedient. This is certainly not a vehicle for winning votes; as a result we are left with the single objective of fighting our own corner.

We as a visible minority must begin to change our outlook and most certainly our philosophy. We must be more collective, in other words we must begin to help ourselves. Our over-dependency on others has brought little gains and much disillusionment. It is imperative that our vision and agenda be altered to match the changing times. Furthermore, if we are to be respected, we must respect ourselves. If we are conscious of the problems we should be capable of acting on them.

I recall in the early sixties how vital it was to develop a community spirit as a means of survival, in order to buy our homes and to extricate ourselves from the rental syndrome but more importantly from evil landlords. Unfortunately, that level of commitment, for multiple reasons seemed to have stagnated. Many of the senior members fell that they have fought their battle and it is time to leave the stage but we still have an important part to play. Our support and advice is invaluable if our offspring are to obtain greater and more significant changes in the society. It is not enough to sit on the sidelines and watch. We have done that long enough. So much so, that it has left us far behind. We are permanently at the bottom end of the political and financial spectrum.

Resistance to our progress is still largely in place. Any advancement is seen as an over abundance of 'political correctness' and is hardly encouraged. Make no mistake, there are many who still feel that our only purpose in this society is to be menial. That we are developing academic, professional and political status in the society still makes uncomfortable reading for some. People are still willing to tell us to 'go back to the jungle'. It is unfortunate that so many folks have not understood the true value of the jungle; a place where Europeans have visited and derived much benefit from. Progress must be determined by ability not skin colour and those with ability must be given the opportunity. Therefore, we must not be distracted from our aims and objectives. Our task in those early days was far from easy. We were able to overcome many obstacles and adversities in order to achieve a measure of success, which can no doubt be invaluable in showing the way forward for our young men and women.

Today we live in a world where advances in technology have taken centre stage. The computer is the new face for change. We are without doubt at a heightened phase of science and medicine and for the young these are exciting times. The pace of society is so great, it has become a serious challenge for older folk like me but what is difficult to understand is why stability is giving way to a state of fear and uncertainty.

In the distant past things were more predictable and measured. A job for life is now a distant memory. The work environment is nowhere as secure as it once was. Hire and fire is a feature that is all too familiar these days and stress and tension has become a significant part of the modern way of living.

In spite of the tremendous progress society has made, there are too many questions left unanswered. For example – why have the barometers that govern discipline seemed to suddenly be eroded?

Why are moral values and standards of decency losing the battle to a yobbish and aggressive culture?

Why have the general public no faith in and have lost all confidence in their politicians?

Why have schools lost so many playing fields, a once vital part of their social development and for nurturing a competitive spirit?

Why in a society of plenty, there is so much poverty? Why do children at the tender age of eight and nine need to carry a mobile phone?

Why have only a limited few Black players, who for thirty years and more, that were involved in the 'beautiful game' of football failed to acquire managerial status?

Why has it become fashionable for the young not to give up their seats to the elderly?

Why has chivalry become a lost art in society?

Why has dressing up seemed to have lost its appeal, especially the presenters on national television?

Why do so many black athletes, who have done brilliantly for their country, seem to disappear from the moment their career comes to an end, as opposed to their white counter parts?

Why do buses run in pairs?

We may never know the answers to some of these questions. Some things change others do not.

In the interim, we are left with the serious and very solemn process of burying our dead. Many of our relatives, friends and colleagues are no more. We had the time of our lives; getting married, baptising our young ones and watching them grow up, what seemed to be not so long ago. Alas, the battle for survival, the struggle that was joined all those years ago, has no doubt taken its toll on so many. We remember them if only for the joy and pleasure we shared in times gone by. There were times we laughed when quite easily we could have cried, and when circumstances and tribulations seemed beyond us, one thing was certain, we could always depend on each other to make our paths a little brighter. For those who are no more, we say thanks a million for the memories.

DREAMS OF HOPE

I shall continue to hope for better things to come. That hope may be fulfilled by the young, the ambitious and those that have the will to win. Life is a challenge that we all have to face and in that great struggle, there are winners and losers. On reflection, I did not aspire to heights that I thought I could accomplish. Nevertheless I hold no brief with the 'what might have been' scenario. In a strange way, fate has been kind to me and life is too short for regrets. I have been blessed with good health and a modicum of intelligence that has served me well over the years. For that I am grateful.

I still have dreams, though they are not of personal attainment or aggrandisement. No, my dreams are merely to see this world of ours becoming a better place than it presently is, that humanity lives and that helping each other has not become a distant and forgotten habit. How wonderful it would be to see the developed world not only making promises but also honouring them.

I dream of the day when we can eliminate mankind's greatest scourge – poverty from the face of this earth, where millions are denied basic clean water and are dying from cholera, dysentery and other dangerous bacterial diseases, when so much of it can be avoided.

I dream of a change in the deadly imbalance of millions of people who are victims of slave labour and are subjected to the horrid and insidious experience of surviving on less than a mere pittance a day.

I dream of a world that is free of pollution. Where due consideration can be given to environmental and atmospheric conditions – climate change – limiting global warming and in doing so, creating a world that is fit for future generations to enjoy.

I dream of rich countries removing their protectionist tariffs and suspending subsidies to their farmers, giving developing nations an opportunity to compete in a world where the political chasm between those that have and those that have not, is so outrageously out of synch.

I dream of the day when a greater degree of wealth will be spent on the advancement of science and medicine and less on the manufacture of guns and ammunitions, especially weapons of mass destruction.

I dream of that wonderful day when wars, riots, animosity and strife can be eliminated from the continent of Africa, giving peace a chance and helping that great continent to rekindle some of its past glory.

I dream of the day when all schools, everywhere, would as a matter of course, include in their curriculum, Africa's history.

I dream of the day when greed and selfishness would be overcome by compassion and goodwill. When respect for all mankind is fully and properly recognised.

I dream of the day when all of us would begin to recognise that 'Black' is a colour and not a race and sincerely hope that people, who continue to disrespect our heritage, realise that they are doing a severe injustice to our people.

I dream of the day when developed countries would stop selling arms to their poorer neighbours, whose limited finances would be better spent alleviating poverty rather than killing each other.

I wholeheartedly dream of the day when the international community would once and for all pay serious attention and move expeditiously to remove this grotesque and evil disease called AIDS, which has created havoc and untold distress to so many millions world-wide.

To ignore the plight of so many and the suffering that this dreadful illness brings, especially to poor countries that are desperately in need of both education and medicines, and are experiencing the worst impact of this dangerous illness, would surely be both morally and ethically indefensible.

In this animal kingdom of ours, we are the only ones who are alive to what is right and what is wrong. We are capable of separating what is evil from what is good. We know how to reason. We are conversant with the quality of logic. Our vision and intellect is beyond compare. The quality of us humans is supreme. Our value system is unique. Therefore, it is simple to deduce that the advantage we enjoy over all else is amazing. It is a supreme gift that we must use for the betterment of mankind.

These dreams are simply impossible dreams, I know - Utopia on Earth - hardly likely.

Unfortunately the ideal World is still many, many millions of light years away. Logic, common sense and sound realistic thinking tells us all not to expect the improbable or the impossible. Yet! The greatest asset that we humans have is ourselves. Ultimately – it is only mankind who can make the impossible possible. Whatever happens in our world is of our own creation.

If humans can create wars, distress and pain, if we are capable of creating horrors of unendurable proportions, if evil, poverty and injustice are man made - then with the best will in the world, we should be able to manufacture PEACE.